BRAINSTRAINS®

POWER PUZZLES

BrainStrains®

POWER PUZZLES

240
MIND-BLOWING
CHALLENGES
OPTICAL ILLUSIONS
TRICKY MYSTERIES
TESTS OF LOGIC
NUMBER MAGIC

Frank Coussement
Peter De Schepper
Keith Kay
Des MacHale
Paul Sloane
Norman D. Willis

STERLING INNOVATION
An imprint of Sterling Publishing Co., Inc.

New York / London
www.sterlingpublishing.com

STERLING and the distinctive Sterling logo are registered trademarks of Sterling Publishing Co., Inc.

10 9 8 7 6 5 4 3 2 1

Published by Sterling Publishing Co., Inc.
387 Park Avenue South, New York, NY 10016
This book is comprised of the following Sterling titles:
BrainStrains® BrainSnack™, Puzzles © 2002 by Frank Coussement & Peter De Schepper
BrainStrains® Great Color Optical Illusions © 2002 by Keith Kay
BrainStrains® Sneaky Lateral Thinking Puzzles © 2002 by Paul Sloane & Des MacHale
BrainStrains® Clever Logic Puzzles © 2002 by Norman D. Willis

Published by Sterling Publishing Co., Inc.
387 Park Avenue South, New York, NY 10016
© 2002 by Sterling Publishing Co., Inc.
Distributed in Canada by Sterling Publishing
c/o Canadian Manda Group, 165 Dufferin Street
Toronto, Ontario, Canada M6K 3H6
Distributed in the United Kingdom by GMC Distribution Services
Castle Place, 166 High Street, Lewes, East Sussex, England BN7 1XU
Distributed in Australia by Capricorn Link (Australia) Pty. Ltd.
P.O. Box 704, Windsor, NSW 2756, Australia

Manufactured in China
All rights reserved

Sterling ISBN-13: 978-1-4027-5401-2
          ISBN-10: 1-4027-5401-9

For information about custom editions, special sales, premium and corporate purchases, please contact Sterling Special Sales Department at 800-805-5489 or specialsales@sterlingpub.com.

Table of Contents

Introduction

BrainStrains™ Power Puzzles will challenge your mind and provide hours of fun mental stimulation. Visual, number, and logic puzzles — and mind-blowing colorful optical illusions — will test, tone, and sharpen your thinking skills. (Please note: when you are doing the Sneaky Lateral Thinking Puzzles you will want to use the puzzle clues which begin on page 315.)

BrainStrains™

BrainSnack™
Puzzles

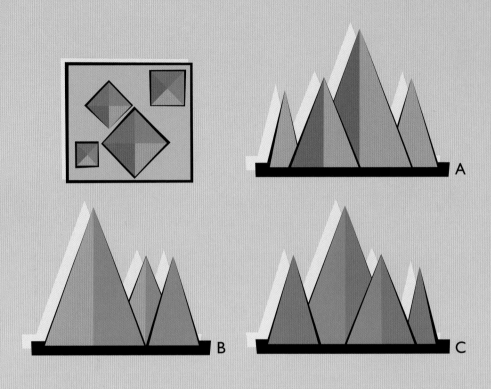

In the upper left corner you will find a floor plan for a mountain. Which mountain landscape (A–C) does not correspond to the plan?

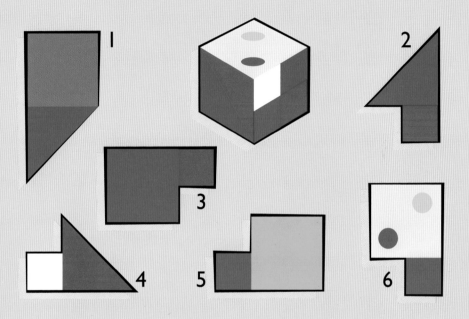

Which piece (1–6) is not needed
to make the cube?

How many glasses of eggnog
did the skier drink during his
2001 skiing holiday?

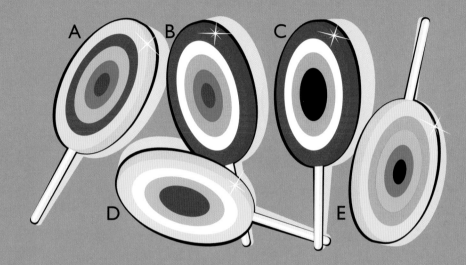

Three out of these five lollipops were
made by the same candy factory.
The factory has only seven different
flavors for their lollipops. Which three
lollipops are theirs?

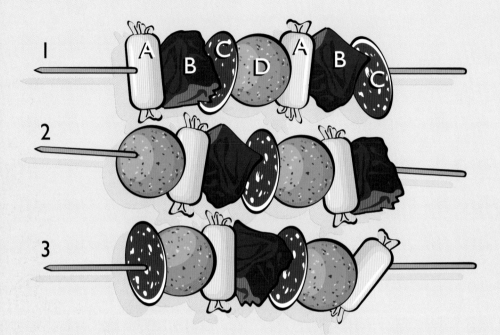

Four different kinds of meat were used to make these skewers consisting of seven pieces of meat. These are the first three skewers of a whole series. What will skewer 99 look like? Your answer will take the form of DABCDAB.

What number should replace
the question mark?

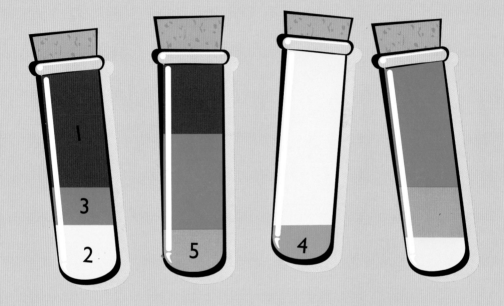

Which liquid (1–5) has
the highest density?

4 4 2 6 2

10 4 28 ?

What number is missing
at the end of this series?

The wrong figures appear on the
display of this broken calculator.
When you enter the numbers 708510,
the numbers 4105282740 actually appear
on the display. How will the numbers
50364 be converted by the calculator?

What print (A–E) has not
been made by the stamp?

Which cube is the same
as the layout on the left?

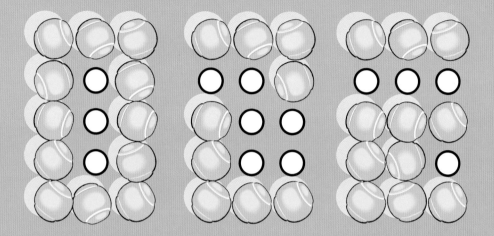

What tennis term do you get by moving one ball in each group?

.

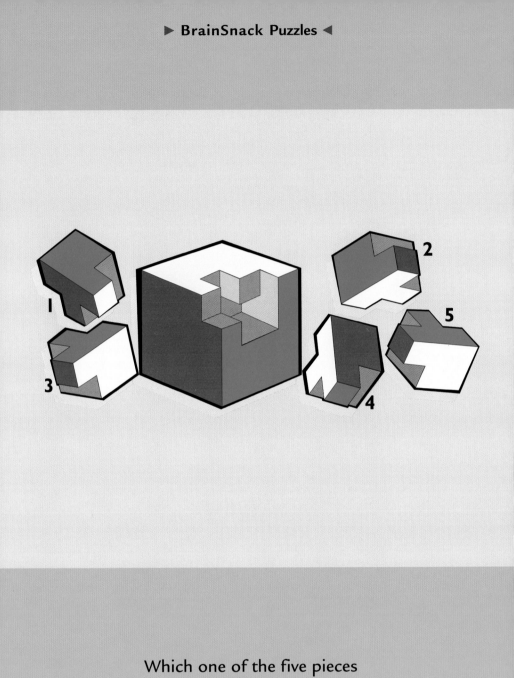

Which one of the five pieces
will complete the block?

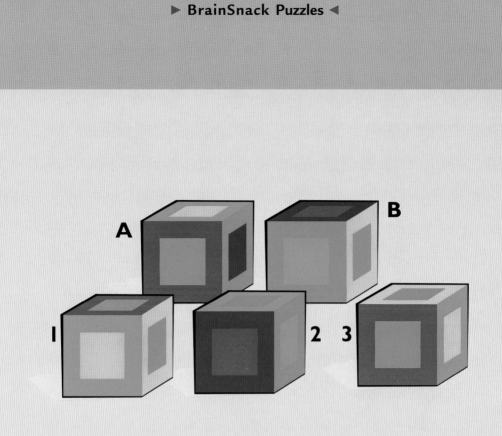

A and B are identical cubes that are
seen from different sides. Therefore,
you see all six sides of the cube.
Which one of the three cubes
(1, 2, or 3) is not a different view
of the original cube?

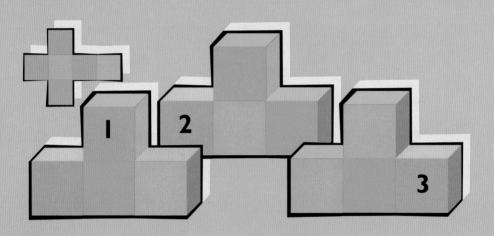

The illustration at the top left is the layout of an unfolded cube. Folding the cube and using it four times produces two out of these three daises. Which dais used a different cube?

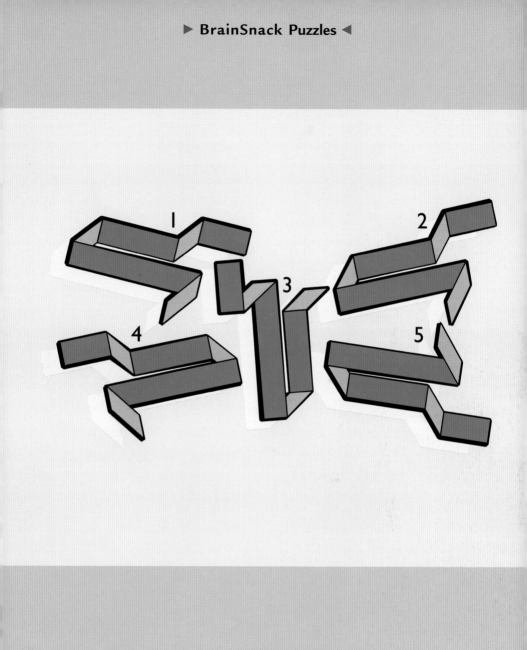

The same ribbon is shown
from different perspectives.
Which ribbon (1–5) is wrong?

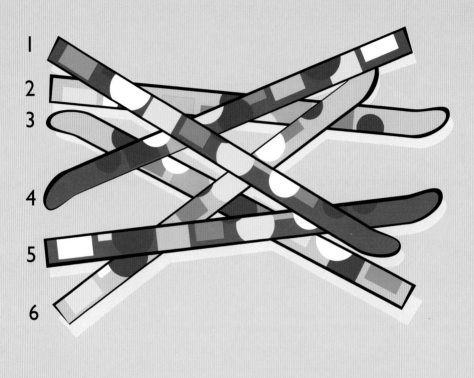

1
2
3
4
5
6

There are three pairs of skis here.
Which numbers make up each pair?

How many eggs are being moved
by this ski lift?

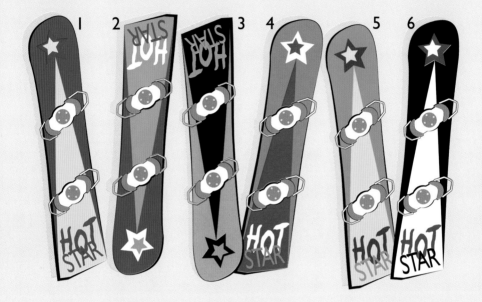

Which snowboard has a
printing design error?

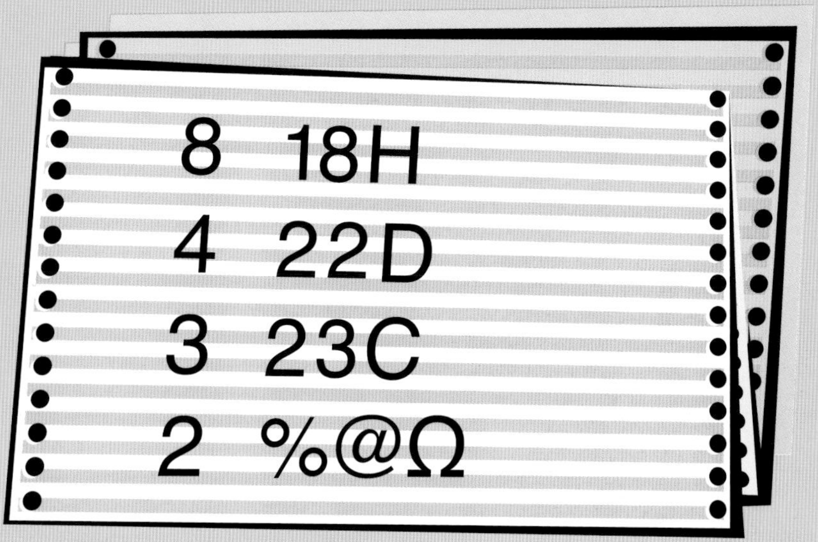

8 18H
4 22D
3 23C
2 %@Ω

When asked to produce a listing of the pin codes for the numbers 8, 4, 3, and 2, the computer made a mistake in the case of a pin code for the number 2. What should be the correct pin code for 2?

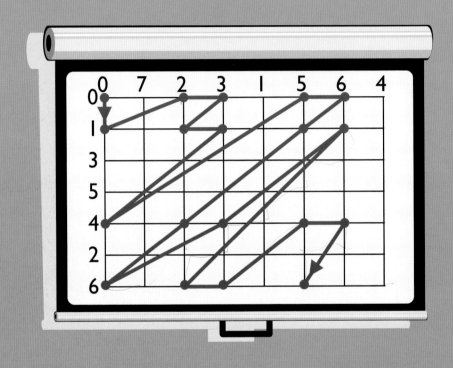

The graph is complete except for the endpoint. Indicate the coordinates of the endpoint by giving first a value of the horizontal axis and then a vertical value.

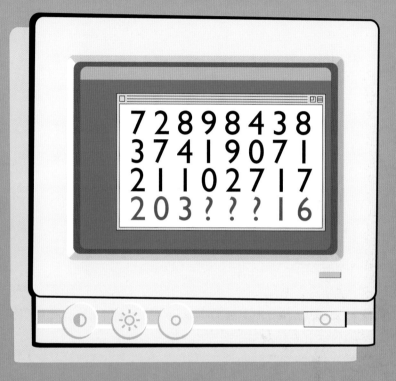

7 2 8 9 8 4 3 8
3 7 4 1 9 0 7 1
2 1 1 0 2 7 1 7
2 0 3 ? ? ? 1 6

What three numbers
are missing?

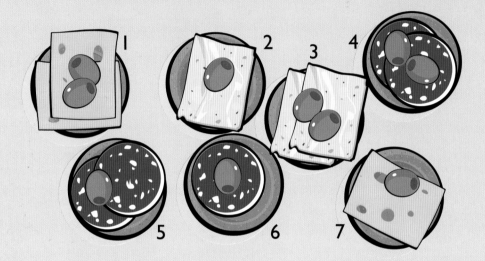

Which serving of bread is
the odd one out?

How many buttons should there be
on the body of the last snowman?

How many berries should
there be on the last holly?

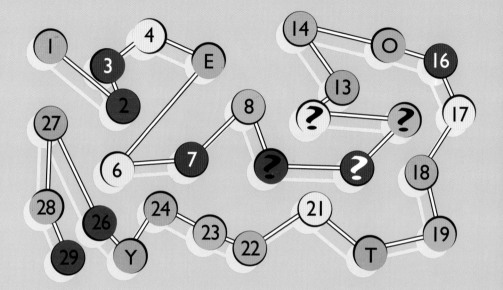

The carnival parade passes through four different points of a city. Which numbers (or letters) should replace the question marks?

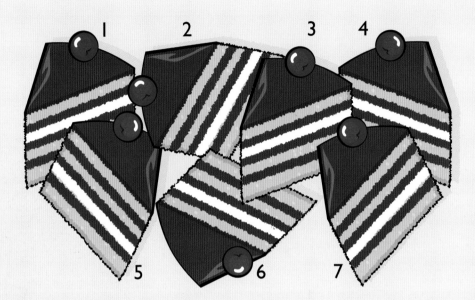

These are slices from three different cakes. There is only one slice from the third cake. Which slice is it?

Which wrapping is
the odd one out?

What coat of arms belongs to
a different family?

Which stack of index cards
is the odd one out?

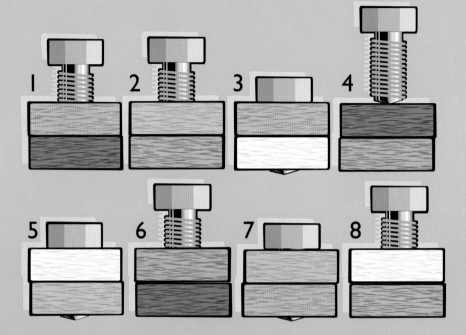

Certain blocks have threaded holes;
others do not. All the blocks of the
same color are identical and all the
threaded bolts are equally long.
Which set of blocks is incorrect?

Which arrow should be on the fifth
key of the second row: L (left),
R (right), LU (left upper), LB
(left bottom), RU (right upper),
or RB (right bottom)?

Which mask does not belong here?

Which flag (1–11) does not belong here?

What number should be on
the next pair of shorts?

What number should replace
the question mark?

Three out of the four caps have been
made by the same company. The
company used four different fabrics.
Which cap didn't it make?

What number should replace
the question mark?

Which object is not identical
to the others?

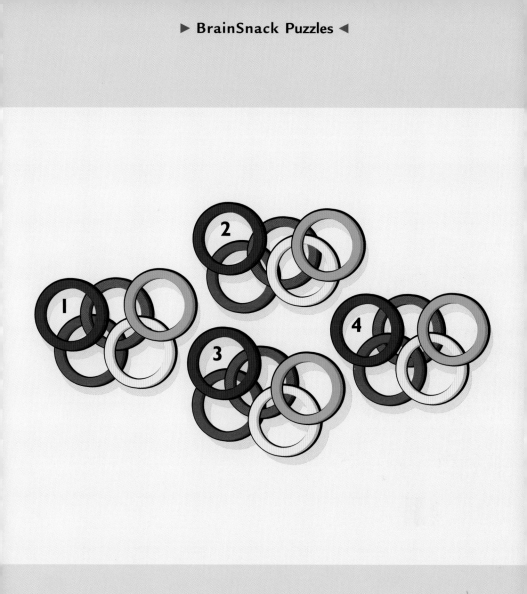

Which design does not belong
in this set?

1822 2142 1914

The price for each set
of medals is shown.
How much does a bronze medal,
which is part of the third set, cost?

The stonemason made a mistake on the design of this frieze. Indicate the row and the position of the mistake. For example, if there is a mistake on the sixth element of series B, the answer would be B6.

How many white dots should there be
on the wings of the last ladybug?

B

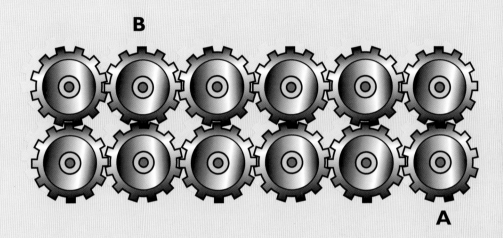

A

If you turn Wheel A clockwise,
which way will Wheel B turn—
to the left (counterclockwise) or to
the right (clockwise)?

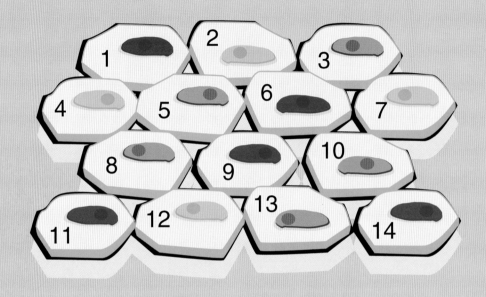

Which is the odd one out?

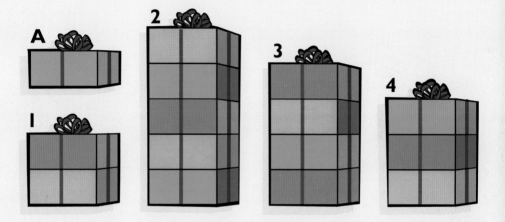

On what pile (1, 2, 3, or 4) is Brian
going to put his last present (A)?

On each side of each cube is printed a different symbol. Each cube has the same six symbols. Which cube (1, 2, 3, or 4) is exactly the same as cube 0?

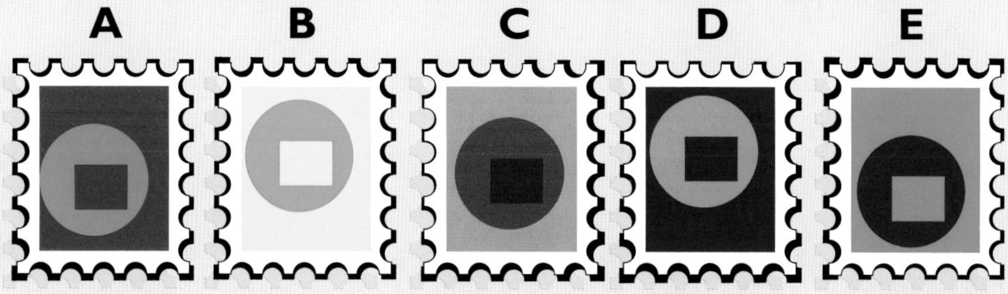

One of the stamps in this series
does not fit in with the others.
Which one is it?

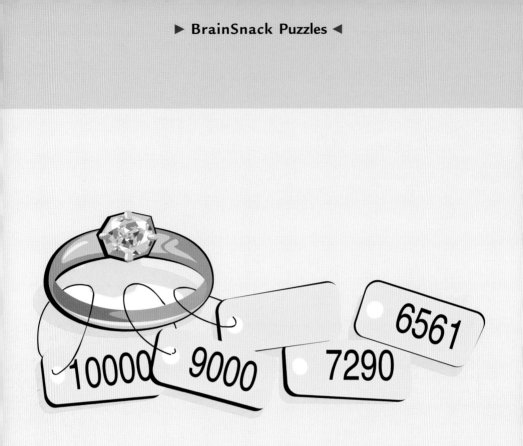

The price of this ring keeps dropping.
What price should be its price on
the third tag?

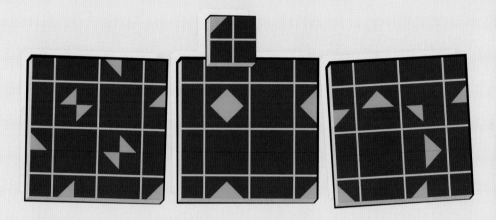

Which of the three large patterns can
be made with the small tile?

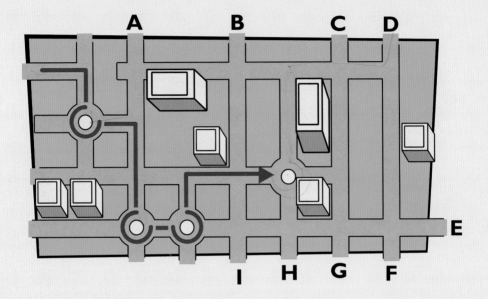

At which exit point will the marathon
runner leave the city?

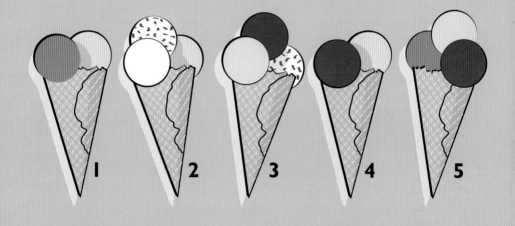

Brian bought four of the five ice creams from his usual ice cream store. The store has only four different flavors. Which ice (1, 2, 3, 4, or 5) did he buy someplace else?

These nine letters of the alphabet belong together for a reason. Once you figure out the reason, find the missing letter.

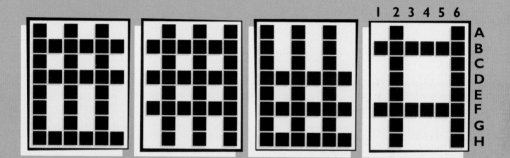

On this digital display, horizontal
and vertical bars are shown.
The bars follow a certain pattern.
The last screen, however, broke down.
Which vertical (1–6) and horizontal
(A–H) bar should be there?

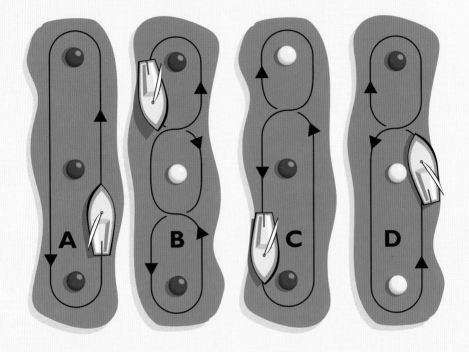

On which sailboat (A, B, C, or D)
did the captain make a track error?

How many points were made
at the fourth basket?

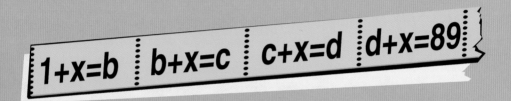

1+x=b   b+x=c   c+x=d   d+x=89

What is the value of x?

Four of the five ladybugs belong to
the same species. Which ladybug is
the odd one out? There can only be at
most four different colors in one
species of ladybug.

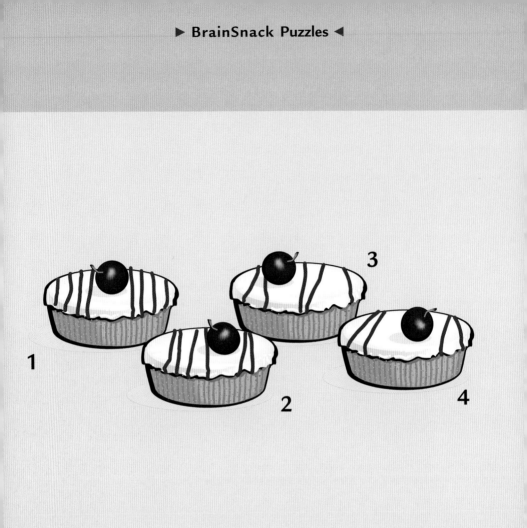

The cakes change each month.
Cake 1 has been made in August,
Cake 2 in June, and Cake 3 in May. In
what month has Cake 4 been made?

The numbers on the keypad follow
a certain logic. What number should
replace the question mark?

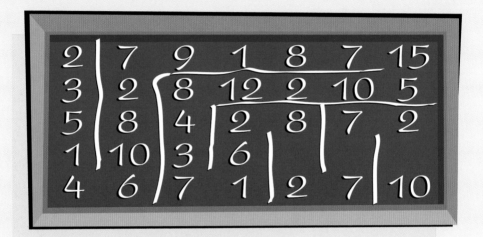

The blackboard shows a series of
numbers. What should the three
missing numbers be?

Move just one single chalk line to
complete the formula.

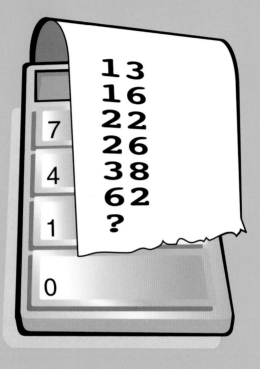

What number should replace
the question mark?

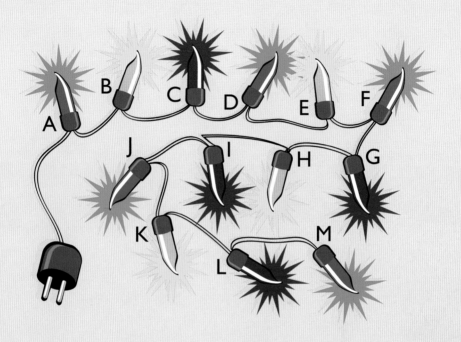

Which two lightbulbs need to
be switched for the lights to follow
a sequence?

How many red Christmas lights
should be on the last tree?

These are all different views of the same die. The last die has a blank side. How many dots should be there?

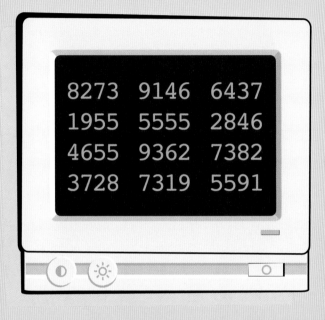

8273 9146 6437
1955 5555 2846
4655 9362 7382
3728 7319 5591

Which number does not
belong here?

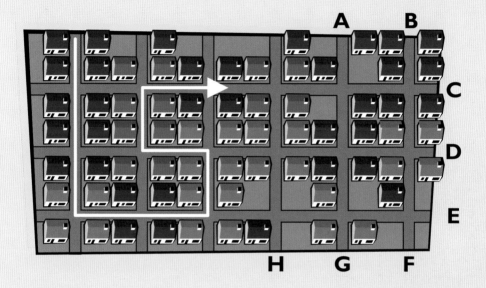

At which exit point will the
messenger leave the city?

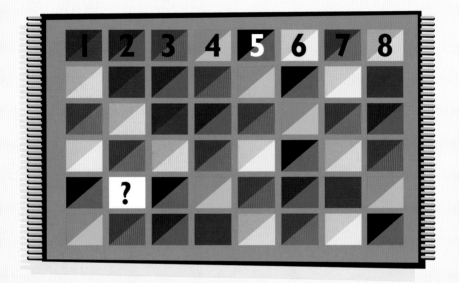

Which piece (1, 2, 3, 4, 5, 6, 7, or 8)
should replace the question mark?

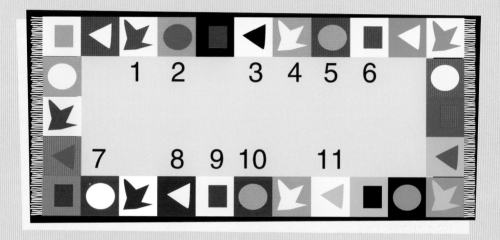

A mistake has been made in the pattern on this carpet. At which section (1–11) did the weaver make his mistake?

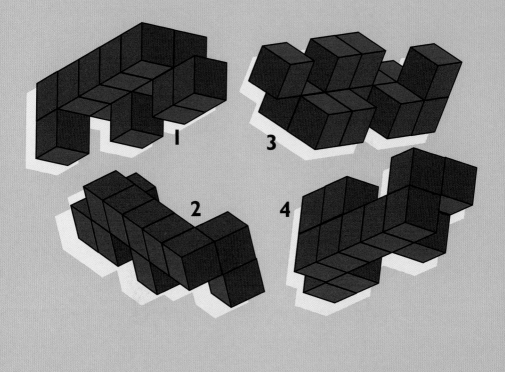

Which two elements constitute
a perfect beam?

In what order should the last set of blocks be stacked? Indicate the numbers of the blocks in your answer (e.g., 122312), starting with the bottom block.

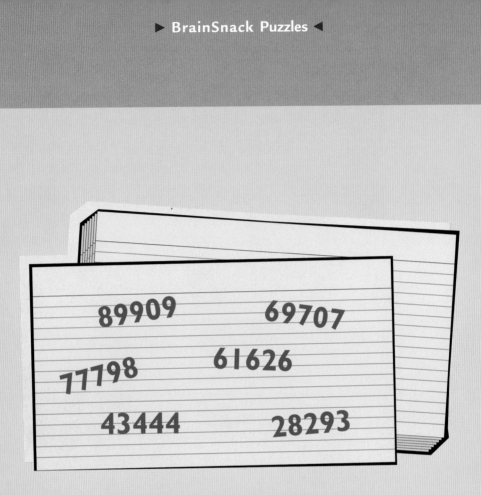

Which number does not fit
with the others?

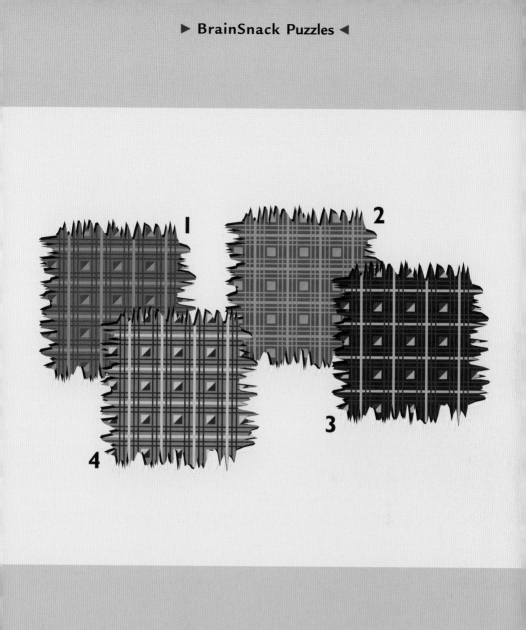

Which piece of fabric does not
belong in the same Scottish family?

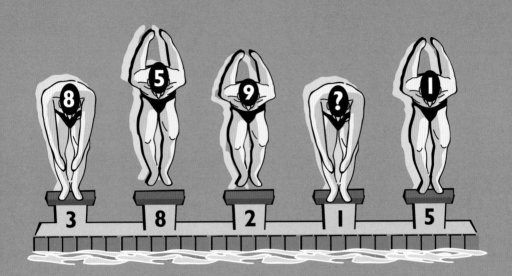

What number should be
on the cap of the swimmer
in lane 1?

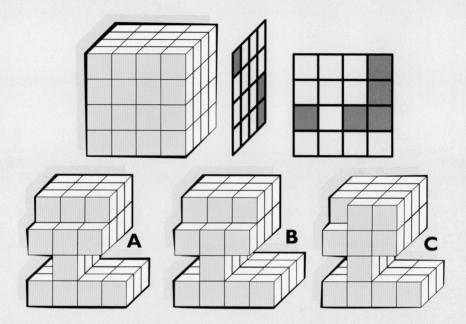

A piece of cheese successively passes through two molds. The cheese can only pass through the white squares. It moves from left to right through the first mold, and then from the back to the front through the second mold. Which piece of cheese will we be left with: A, B, or C ?

$$\frac{3}{4} \quad \frac{4}{3} \quad \frac{6}{8} \quad \frac{24}{18} \quad \frac{72}{96} \quad \frac{?}{?}$$

What fraction will complete
the series?

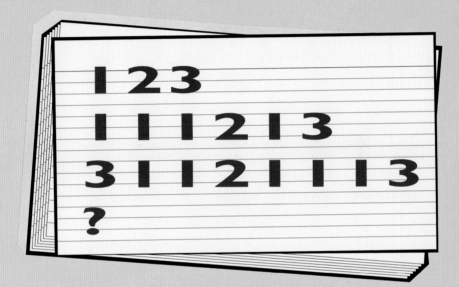

What will be the sequence of
numbers on the last line?

Just as in genetics, we find ourselves in the presence of dominants. Which element (1, 2, 3, or 4) is the result of the third operation?

This calculator is broken. The numbers on the keypad do not correspond with what appears on the display. If you press the numbers 4572301, the screen shows 1542630. If we press the number 89 on the keypad, what number will show up on the screen?

BrainStrains™

Great Color
Optical
Illusions

What do you see in this strange picture?

Is the zebra black with white stripes or
is it white with black stripes?

Slowly rotate this page in a circular motion. What happens to the clown's drum? What's unusual about the word "rotator"?

The name of this old-time print is
"Time Passes." Why do you think it
was given this title?

Can you figure out why this picture is
titled "Before and After Marriage"?

This picture shows a young girl and
her grandmother. Can you find both
of them?

How can you get the bee to move
closer to the flower?

Place a pencil along the line of the two arrows.
What happens to the color of the circle?

What playing card is represented in
this illustration?

Stare at the red dot for about 30
seconds. Try not to blink. Then look
at a blank wall or a sheet of white
paper. You will see a famous lady.
Who is she?

MADAM I'M ADAM

Do you notice anything unusual about this
eaten apple? The clue is in the phrase.
What's unusual about the phrase?

This is a real postage stamp of Daniel Webster. If you turn it upside down and look very carefully, you will see someone else. Who do you see?

Can you figure out what these shapes represent?

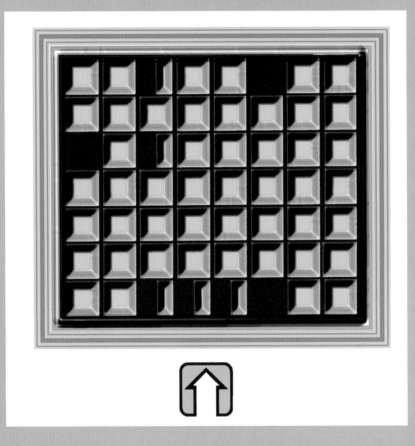

Can you discover the secret word that
has been concealed in this design?

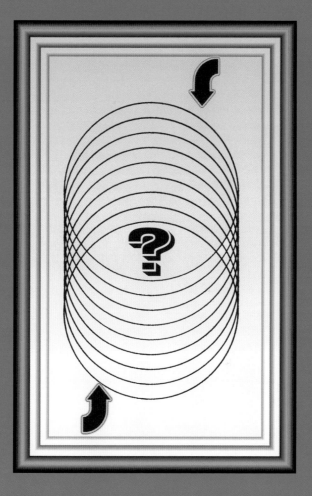

You can look through this coil
from either end. Keep staring at it
and what happens?

Otto is holding a cake. One slice is missing. Can you find it? There is also something odd about the name "Otto." What is it?

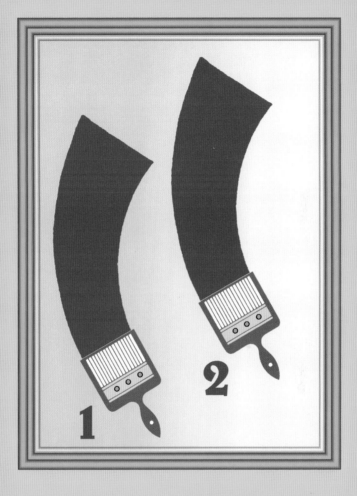

Are these two painted stripes exactly
the same size, or is one bigger than
the other?

What's so special about
this set of numbers?

What do you see in this picture:
Blue arrows or yellow arrows?

What do you see in this picture?

What is this a picture of?

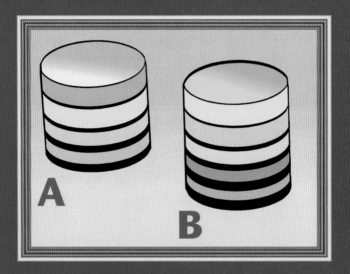

Which pile of disks has the same
height and width?

This soldier is looking for his horse.
Do you have any idea where it is?

What happens when you rotate this
page in a circular motion?

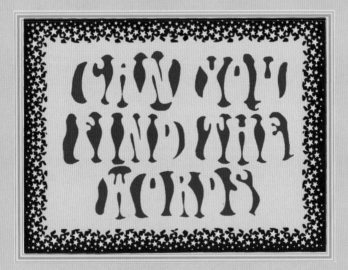

Can you find the hidden message?
What does it say?

The soldier is pointing his finger straight
at you. Move your head from left to
right. What appears to happen?

Can you find this baby's mother?

This old sketch is called
"Under the Mistletoe."
What's odd about this drawing?

The sailor is looking through his
telescope to find his girlfriend. Can
you find her?

This is a picture of the Roman god Bacchus. If you look very carefully you will also see a picture of Romeo and Juliet. Can you find them?

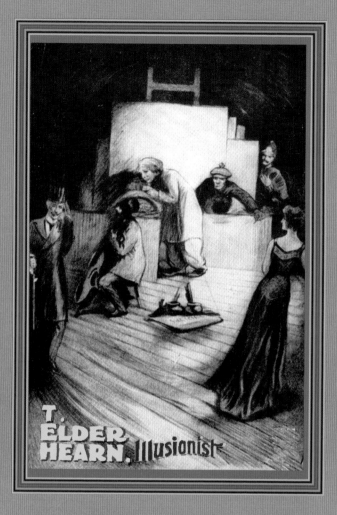

This is a poster of vaudeville performer, T. Elder Hearn. He was a quick-change artist. What do you see in this publicity print?

This mathematical problem is wrong.
How can you correct it?

Sherlock Holmes is reading a
headline. What does it say?
Are you sure?

The brown shapes may seem
unrelated, but they form a figure. It is
an example of a "closure." Can you
see what the figure is?

What do you see, purple glasses
or green vases?

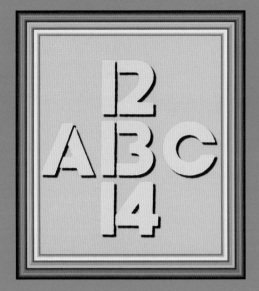

What do you see in the middle of the frame?
Is it the letter B or the number 13?

Does this sign say "knowledge" or
does it say "ignorance"?

The shop was selling poor-quality dice at 50¢ each.
This was not the correct price. Can you
figure out what was the real price?

How can you get the boy to take a
spoonful of his medicine?

At first glance, we see a pig.
But where is the farmer?

Observe this cow very carefully.
Do you notice anything unusual about it?

Read the words in the hat very slowly.
What do they say?

Using only your eyes, count the
number of F's in the above sentence.
How many are there?

Can you spot the farmer in this landscape?

Can you see where Napoleon is hiding?

Napoleon's supporters used to wear
violets as a sign of their allegiance.
This print hides the faces of Napoleon,
Maria Louisa, and the young king of
Rome. Can you find them?

This attractive landscape print holds a secret.
Can you find the landlord?

This is the island of St. Helena.
Where is Napoleon?

Can you discover why this old British
colonial patriotic design is called
"The Glory of a Lion Is His Mane"?

What is unusual about
this sentence?

What is strange about these donkeys?

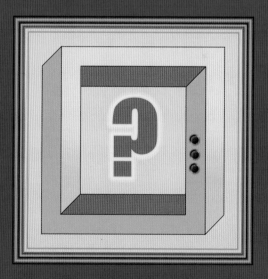

Are the three dots on the inside or the
outside of this frame?

Can you see what's wrong
with this poster?

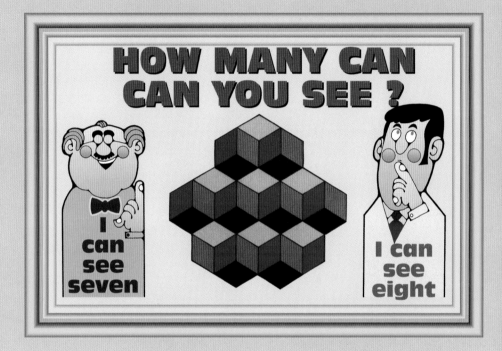

How many cubes can you see,
seven or eight?

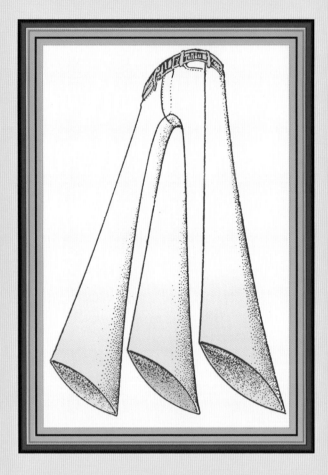

Can you see what's wrong with
this pair of bell-bottoms?

What's wrong with this picture?

The farmer's son was adding up
the large number of eggs laid over a
3-week period. Do you see anything
unusual about the answer?

Turn the page upside down and you will
see that the year 1961 still says 1961.
When was the last "upside down" year
and when will the next one occur?

A farmer put up this sign. Can you understand what he was trying to say?

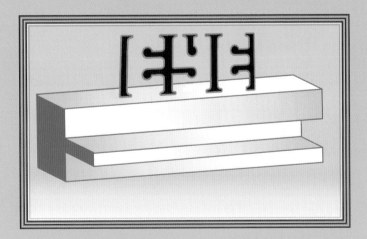

Can you figure out the meaning of the shapes on the top shelf? And what's unusual about the structure?

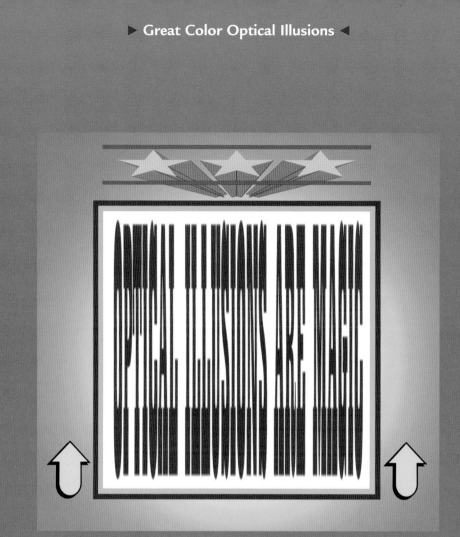

Can you read this secret message?
Tilt the page to eye level and look
in the direction of the arrows with
one eye closed.

Stare at the yellow dot for about 30 seconds.
Try not to blink. Now stare at a piece of
white paper. What do you see?

Clowns work in the circus. Here's the
clown. Where's the circus?

What bird do you see here,
a hawk or a goose?

Look carefully at this dog.
Can you find its master?

Can you figure out what this Victorian
puzzle shows? Is it an animal,
vegetable, or mineral? Try looking
at it from different angles.

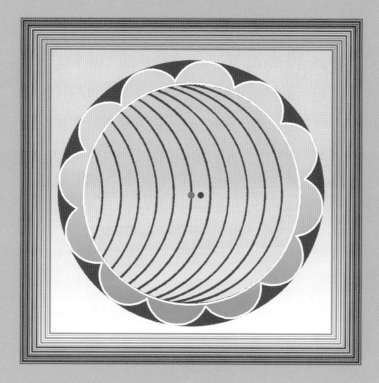

Which of these two dots
is in the true center?

Do you notice anything unusual
about this flight of steps?

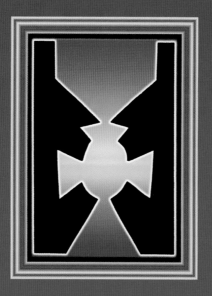

What do you see in this picture?

Is the star closer to the top or
the base of the mountain?

Magician Horace Goldin used this flyer to advertise his theater shows. Who looks taller, Goldin as a man or as a boy?

Will the girl ever get to the bottom step on this flight of stairs?

Without turning the page upside
down, describe this man. Is he happy
or sad? Now check to find out.

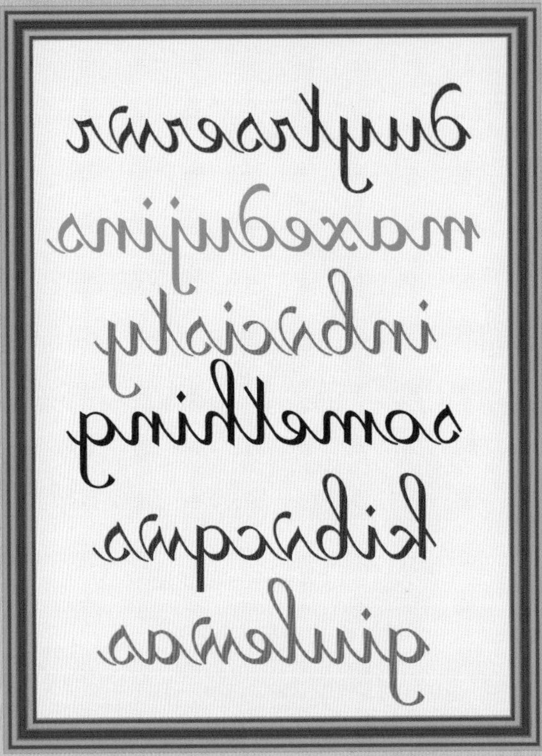

Only one of these sets of letters says
something when viewed in a mirror.
Can you figure out which one it is
before using the mirror?

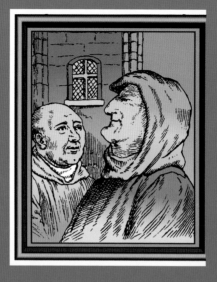

The hooded monk has a bizarre
secret. What is it?

How do you turn a duck into a rabbit?

This picture is based on what were known in Victorian times as "Fantasy Faces." What do you see?

Is there life after death?

In just one move, can you make the matches
form a complete oblong shape?

We hope that you have enjoyed the optical illusions in this book. Now, a final thought. To find out what happens to all good things, just turn this page upside down.

Sneaky
Lateral
Thinking
Puzzles

A penniless sculptor made a
beautiful metal statue, which he
sold. Because of this he died
soon afterward. Why?

A man was preparing a fish to eat for a meal when he made a mistake. He then knew that he would shortly die. How?

A foreign visitor to London
wanted to ride up the escalator
at the subway station, but did
not do so. Why?

A golfer dreamed all his life of getting a hole in one. However, when he eventually did get a hole in one, he was very unhappy and, in fact, quit golf altogether. Why?

Why did a man write
the same two letters
over and over again on
a piece of paper?

What major scientific
blunder did Shakespeare
include in his play
Twelfth Night?

Why did the fashion for
silk hats in the U.S. lead to
an increase in the number
of small lakes and bogs?

The ancient Greek playwright
Aeschylus was killed by a
tortoise. How?

A man stole a very expensive car
owned by a very rich woman.
Although he was a very good driver,
within a few minutes he was involved
in a serious accident. Why?

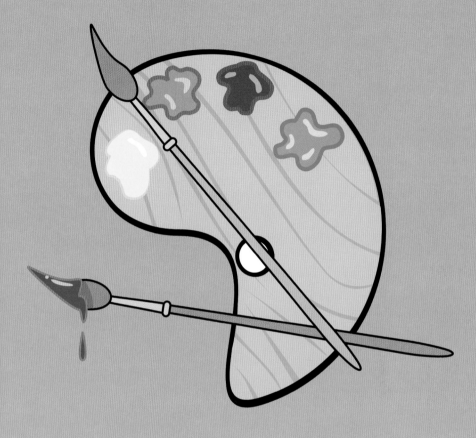

Leonardo da Vinci created some
secret designs for his paintings
that he did not want anyone to
see. He hid them, but they were
recently discovered. How?

Why did a woman send out
1,000 anonymous Valentine
cards to different men?

A man was driving down the road into town with his family on a clear day. He saw a tree and immediately stopped the car and then reversed at high speed. Why?

A mall café is pestered by teenagers who come in, buy a single cup of coffee, and stay for hours, and thus cut down on available space for other customers. How does the owner get rid of them, quite legally?

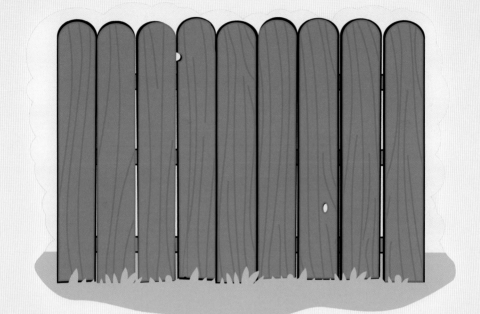

A man painted his garden fence green
and then went on holiday. When he
came back two weeks later, he was
amazed to see that the fence was
blue. Nobody had touched the fence.
What had happened?

A man, a woman, and a child are watching a train come into a station. "Here it comes," says the man. "Here she comes," says the woman. "Here he comes," says the child. Who was correct?

Why did the vicar only want
a black dog?

A runner was awarded a prize for
winning a marathon. But the judges
disqualified him when they saw a
picture of his wristwatch. Why?

Why are two little animals
alone in a little boat in the
middle of the ocean?

A famous dancer was found
strangled. The police did not
suspect murder. Why not?

A man standing in the middle of a
solid concrete floor dropped a tomato
six feet, but it did not break or bruise.
How come?

A little shop in New York is called
The Seven Bells, yet it has eight bells
hanging outside. Why?

A man bought a pair of shoes that were in good condition and that fit him well. He liked the style and they looked good. However, after he had worn them for one day he took them back to the shop and asked for a refund. Why?

A man who was paralyzed in his arms, legs, and mouth, and unable to speak a word, wrote a best-selling book. How?

During fall, a little girl was in her backyard trying to stick the fallen leaves back onto the trees with glue. Why?

A woman heard a tune which she
recognized. She took a gun and shot
a stranger. Why?

A police officer was sitting on his motorcycle at a red traffic light when two teenagers in a sports car drove by him at 50 miles per hour. He did not chase them or try to apprehend them. Why not?

There is an orange in the middle of a
circular table. Without touching or
moving the orange or the table, how
could you place a second orange
under the first?

A young woman applied for a job as a secretary and typist. There were dozens of applicants. The woman could type only eleven words per minute, yet she got the job. Why?

A change in the law in Italy resulted in large sales of white T-shirts with black bands on them. How come?

A man uses a stick to strike a part
of an elephant and after a few
seconds it disappears. The man is
then a lot richer. Why?

A man was building a house when it collapsed all around him. He wasn't injured or upset, and he calmly started to rebuild it. What was going on?

A meteorologist was replaced in
his job because of a stuffed cloud.
What's a stuffed cloud?

A keen ornithologist saw a rare bird that he had never seen before, except in illustrations. However, he was very upset. Then he was frightened. Why?

A horse walked all day. Two of its
legs traveled 21 miles and two legs
traveled 20 miles. How come?

Four people were playing cards.
One played a card and another player
immediately jumped up and started to
take her clothes off. Why?

A farmer has two pigs that are identical twins from the same litter. However, when he sells them he gets 100 times more for one than the other. Why?

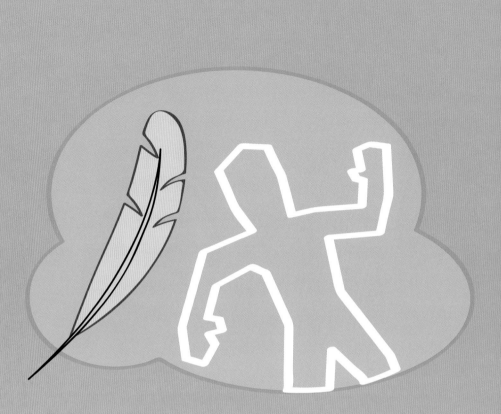

A man lies dead next to a
feather that caused his death.
What happened?

A man bought a beautiful and appropriate wedding gift for a friend's wedding. The gift was wrapped and sent. When the gift was opened at the wedding, the man was highly embarrassed. Why?

Adam was jealous of Brenda's use of a computer. He changed that by means of a hammer. After that, he could use the computer, but Brenda could not. What did he do?

There is a reason why men's clothes
have buttons on the right while
women's have buttons on the left.
What is it?

Two frogs fell into a large cylindrical tank of liquid and both fell to the bottom. The walls were sheer and slippery. One frog died but one survived. How?

A butterfly fell down and a man
was seriously injured. Why?

Why did a man who knew
the time and had two accurate
watches phone a clock that
speaks the time?

A man who did not like cats
bought some fresh salmon and
cream for a cat. Why?

A man undressed to go to bed
and hundreds of people lost
their jobs. Why?

A New York City hairdresser recently said that he would rather cut the hair of three Canadians than one New Yorker. Why?

A man is crowned king. Shortly
afterwards, he is captured by enemy
forces and chopped in two. Why?

Every time he performed in public, it was a complete flop. Yet he became famous for it, and won medals and prizes. People came from all over and paid to see him perform. Who was he?

Why has no one climbed the largest
known extinct volcano?

Because it was raining, the firemen
hosed down the road. Why?

In a very exclusive restaurant several dozen diners are eating a top-class meal upstairs. Downstairs, precisely the same meal is being served at the same number of empty places where there is nobody to eat it. What is going on?

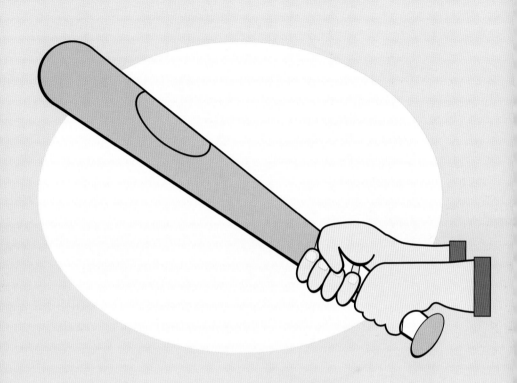

Why did a woman take
a baseball bat and break
her husband's fingers?

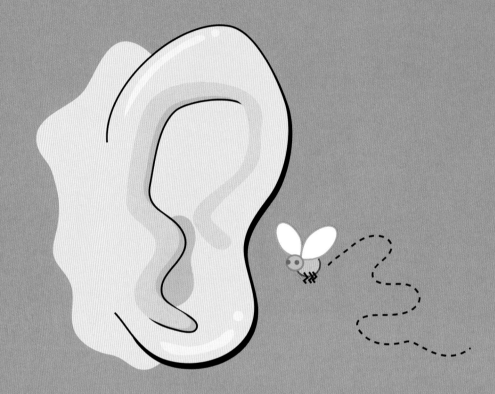

An insect flying into a girl's ear terrifies her. Her mother rushes the girl to the doctor, but he is unable to remove the insect. Suddenly, the mother has an idea. What is it?

BrainStrains™

Clever
Logic
Puzzles

Dragons of Lidd and Wonk

There are few dragons in the kingdom of Lidd, and they have been put on the endangered species list.

Dragons are of two types. Some have reasoned that devouring domestic animals and their owners is, in the long run, not healthy for dragons. They are known as rationals. Some dragons, on the other hand, are reluctant to give up their traditional ways, nor do they fear humans. They are known as predators. The king has decreed that rational dragons shall be protected. Knights caught slaying a rational dragon are dealt with severely.

In addition to being rationals or predators, dragons in Lidd are of two different colors related to their veracity. Gray rational dragons always tell the truth; red rationals always lie. Red predators always tell the truth; gray predators always lie.

There is something appealing to a dragon about being in a land in which knights are not constantly trying to build their reputations by slaying them. It was not surprising, therefore, that the blue dragons from the adjacent land of Wonk began appearing in the kingdom of Lidd. Blue dragons are rationals or predators, but they all lie.

To tell if a dragon is protected, it would help to know its color. However, there is an affliction endemic to humans in Lidd: they are color-blind. To them, all dragons look gray.

One Dragon

A dragon is approached by a knight looking for adventure. The dragon, asked his color and type, responds as follows:

Dragon: I am either blue or gray.

What type is the dragon?

Two Dragons

Two armed knights confront two
dragons, each of whom is asked his color
and type. Their answers follow:

A. 1. I am from Wonk.
    2. B and I are both predators.
B 1. A is not from Wonk, but I am.
    2. I am a rational.

What color and type is each dragon?

Three Dragons

A knight in armor cautiously approaches three dragons who offer the following information:

A. 1. C is from Wonk.
    2. I am not a red predator.
B. 1. A is from Wonk.
    2. A and C are both rationals.
C. 1. B is from Wonk.
    2. B is a predator.

What is the color and type of each dragon?

Two Are from Wonk

A knight confronts three dragons, exactly two of whom are known to be blue dragons from Wonk, and asks each his color and type. Their answers follow:

A. 1. B is from Wonk.
     2. I am a rational.
B. 1. C is from Wonk.
     2. I am a rational.
C. I am a rational.

What color and type is each dragon?

One Dragon from Wonk

Three dragons, exactly one of whom is blue, provide the following information:

A. 1. C is a gray rational.
    2. I am a gray rational.
B. 1. A is a predator.
    2. A is blue.
    3. I am a rational.
C. 1. A is not gray.
    2. B is from Wonk.

What color and type is each dragon?

Three Dragons Again

A lone knight nervously approaches three
dragons, at least one of whom
is from Wonk. They volunteer the
following information:

A. 1. I am either red or gray.
    2. C and I are the same color.
B. 1. A is not red.
    2. C is blue.
C. 1. A's statements are false.
    2. B is not a rational.

What color and type is each dragon?

How Many Are Protected?

A knight looking for a dragon to slay confronts three. He asks each about his color and type. Their answers follow:

A. 1. I am gray.
    2. We three are protected by the king's decree.
    3. C is red.
B. 1. I am not protected by the king's decree.
    2. C is gray.
C. 1. A and I are not the same type.
    2. A is red.
    3. B is a rational.

What color and type is each dragon?

Who Speaks for Whom?

Three dragons respond to a very wary knight as follows:

A. 1. If asked, B would claim that C is a predator.
   2. I am gray.
   3. B is a rational.
B. 1. If asked, C would claim that A is a rational.
   2. C is red.
C. 1. If asked, A would claim that B is red.
   2. A is gray.

What color and type is each dragon?

The Trials of Xanthius

*Among the ancient Greeks, the people of
Athens led all others in their mental acuity.
The gods created a series of trials to test the
Athenians' reasoning ability, as well as their
courage (and perhaps to amuse themselves).
As an incentive, they provided a fabulous
treasure to be won by whoever was successful
in passing every trial.*

   *The trials involved following a path through
a dense forest, across a large savanna, and up
a tall mountain, with choices to be made at*

four points. There was to be no turning back once the challenge was accepted, and no retracing of steps at any time. Dire consequences awaited a challenger who made an incorrect judgment.

No citizen of Athens desired to accept the risk until Xanthius, a young student of Socrates, accepted the challenge.

The First Trial

Hardly had Xanthius entered the forest on the designated path, when it branched into two. He was told that this was the first trial and that one way led to the second trial, while the other led near the domain of a giant serpent, for which he would undoubtedly become a meal. A sign at each path gave instruction.

However, Xanthius was informed that at least one of the signs was false. The signs read as follows:

A

THIS PATH LEADS
TO THE SERPENT.

B

THE SIGN AT
PATH A IS TRUE.

Which path is the one Xanthius should follow?

The Second Trial

Xanthius chose the correct path and, after proceeding into the forest for some time, he came to a branching of the path into three paths. He was informed that one path led to the third trial, while the other two led deep into the forest and eventually into large circles, to which there was no end. Xanthius was told that of the signs at the three paths, two were true and one was false. The signs follow:

A

THE SIGN AT
PATH B IS TRUE.

B

PATH A IS NOT THE
ONE TO FOLLOW.

C

THIS IS THE PATH
TO FOLLOW.

Which path is the one to follow?

The Third Trial

Again, Xanthius chose correctly and proceeded farther into the forest before the path branched into three more paths. His information this time was that one path led to the fourth trial. The other two led over large hidden pits that could not be avoided, and from which escape would be impossible. Xanthius was told that one of the signs at the three paths was false, and two were true. They read as follows:

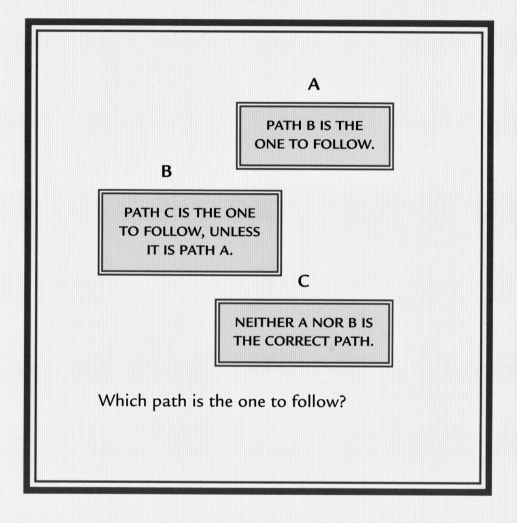

A

PATH B IS THE
ONE TO FOLLOW.

B

PATH C IS THE ONE
TO FOLLOW, UNLESS
IT IS PATH A.

C

NEITHER A NOR B IS
THE CORRECT PATH.

Which path is the one to follow?

The Fourth Trial

Xanthius, having made the correct judgment, followed the path until he came to a deep ravine over which were three bridges. He was told that only one of these could carry him over the ravine. The other two would crumble when he was halfway across, dropping him onto the jagged rocks far below. He was informed that two of the three signs at the three bridges were false, and one was true. The three signs follow:

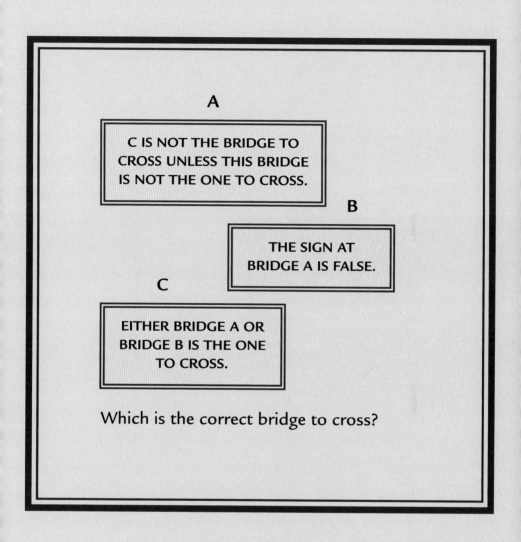

A

C IS NOT THE BRIDGE TO
CROSS UNLESS THIS BRIDGE
IS NOT THE ONE TO CROSS.

B

THE SIGN AT
BRIDGE A IS FALSE.

C

EITHER BRIDGE A OR
BRIDGE B IS THE ONE
TO CROSS.

Which is the correct bridge to cross?

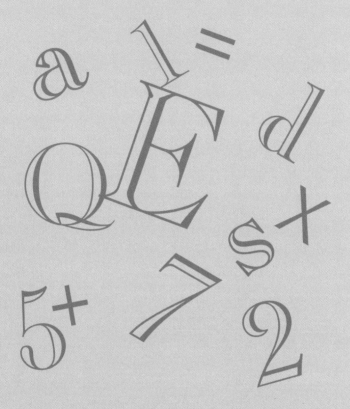

Problems from the Addled Arithmetician

Letters and numbers—to the Addled Arithmetician they are much the same thing. At least it appears so, as he has them reversed.

In this section you will find addition, subtraction, and multiplication problems that he has prepared. Your challenge is to replace the letters with the correct digit. (A zero never appears as the left-most digit of a number.)

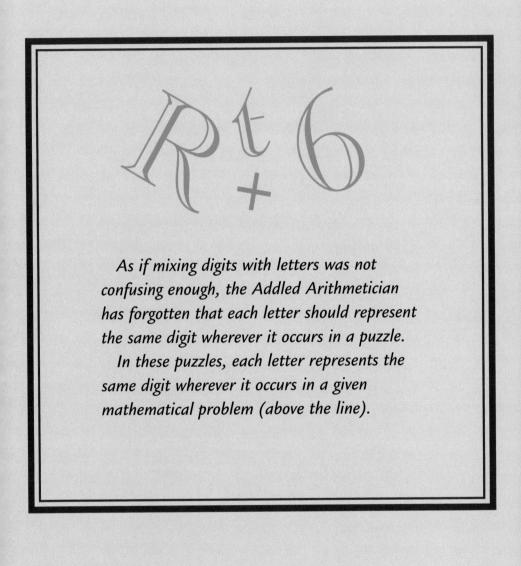

As if mixing digits with letters was not confusing enough, the Addled Arithmetician has forgotten that each letter should represent the same digit wherever it occurs in a puzzle.

In these puzzles, each letter represents the same digit wherever it occurs in a given mathematical problem (above the line).

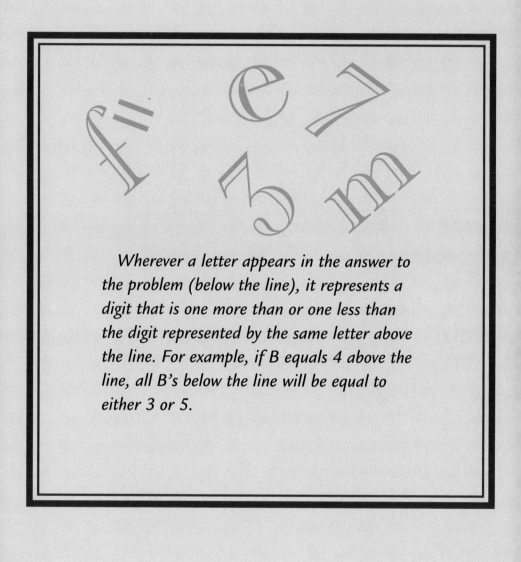

Wherever a letter appears in the answer to the problem (below the line), it represents a digit that is one more than or one less than the digit represented by the same letter above the line. For example, if B equals 4 above the line, all B's below the line will be equal to either 3 or 5.

Addition, Six Digits

Each letter above the line represents a digit that has a difference of one from the digit represented by the same letter below the line.
   The digits are 0, 1, 2, 3, 4, and 5.

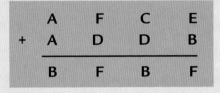

What digit or digits are represented by each letter?

Subtraction, Six Digits

Each letter above the line represents a digit that has a difference of one from the digit represented by the same letter below the line.

The digits are 0, 1, 2, 3, 4, and 5.

	F	B	A	C	B
−	D	A	F	E	B
		C	F	D	E

What digit or digits are represented by each letter?

Addition, Seven Digits

Each letter above the line in this puzzle represents a digit that has a difference of one from the digit represented by the same letter below the line.

The digits are 0, 1, 2, 3, 4, 5, and 6.

	D	G	A	E	C
+	E	F	B	A	C
C	F	G	D	G	F

What digit or digits does each letter represent?

f6sz3

Addition,
Seven Digits Again

Each letter above the line represents a digit that has a difference of one from the digit represented by the same letter below the line.

The digits are: 0, 1, 2, 3, 4, 8, and 9.

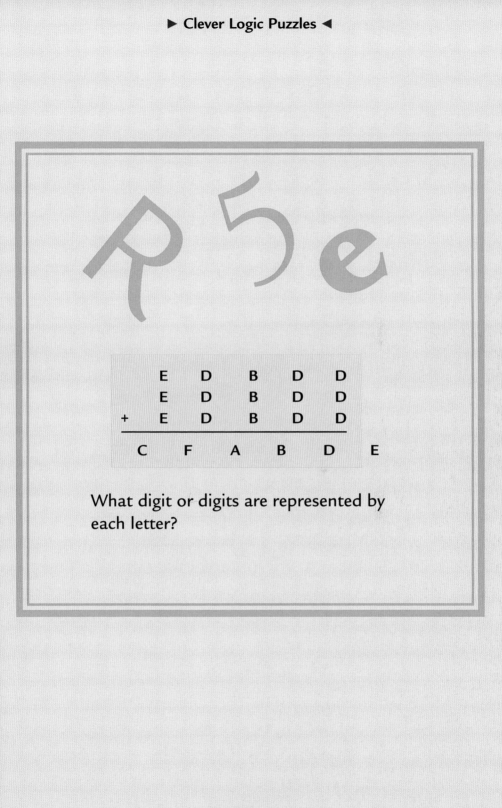

```
      E    D    B    D    D
      E    D    B    D    D
 +    E    D    B    D    D
  ─────────────────────────
   C  F    A    B    D        E
```

What digit or digits are represented by each letter?

sA6m5

Multiplication, Six Digits

Each letter in the multiplication problem
(above the top line) represents a digit
that has a difference of one from the digit
represented by the same letter in the
answer to the problem (below the top
line).

The digits are 0, 1, 2, 3, 4, and 5.

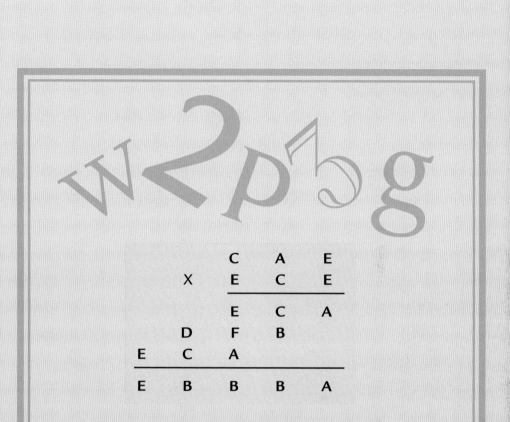

		C	A	E
X		E	C	E
		E	C	A
	D	F	B	
E	C	A		
E	B	B	B	A

What digit or digits are represented by each letter?

Subtraction, Seven Digits

Each letter above the line represents a digit that has a difference of one from the digit represented by the same letter below the line.

The digits are 0, 1, 2, 3, 4, 5, and 6.

	B	D	C	A	B	F	B
−	E	E	B	G	E	A	E
		G	E	E	F	C	F

What digit or digits does each letter represent?

The Land of Liars

In the Land of Liars the inhabitants are all liars, but not all the time. There are those who speak the truth in the morning and lie in the afternoon. The inhabitants in this group are known as Amtrus. There are also those who speak the truth in the afternoon and lie in the morning. The inhabitants in this group are known as Pemtrus.

Your challenge in each puzzle is to identify the Amtrus and the Pemtrus, and to determine if it is morning or afternoon.

Two Inhabitants

Two inhabitants are known to be an Amtru, who speaks the truth only in the morning, and a Pemtru, who speaks the truth only in the afternoon. A makes the following statement:

A. B is the Amtru.

Is it morning or afternoon; which one is the Amtru and which one is the Pemtru?

Two Inhabitants Again

Two inhabitants are asked the time of day. The two are known to be an Amtru, who speaks the truth only in the morning, and a Pemtru, who speaks the truth only in the afternoon. They respond as follows:

A. It is morning.
B. A is the Pemtru.

Is it morning or afternoon; which one is the Amtru and which one is the Pemtru?

Two Inhabitants Once Again

This time, little is known as to the group or groups of the two individuals who make the statements that follow:

A. B and I are Amtrus.
B. A is a Pemtru.

Is it morning or afternoon; and what group or groups do the two speakers represent?

Three Inhabitants

This time three inhabitants are approached. Two are known to be Amtrus, and one is known to be a Pemtru. They volunteer the following statements:

A. B is the Pemtru.
B. C is an Amtru.
C. A is the Pemtru.

Is it morning or afternoon; which two are the Amtrus and which one is the Pemtru?

Three Inhabitants Again

Three inhabitants are asked the time of day. Two are Pemtrus and one is an Amtru. They respond as follows:

A. If asked, B would claim it is morning.
B. If asked, C would claim it is morning.
C. If asked, A would claim it is afternoon.

Is it morning or afternoon; which inhabitants belong to which groups?

The Cases of Inspector Detweiler

There are some within Inspector Detweiler's shire who do not always obey the laws. This extraordinary sleuth has been faced with several crimes that require solving. Your challenge is to determine which suspects are telling the truth and which are not, and who are the guilty.

Who Stole the Stradivarius?

A famous violinist was in town for a concert. While he was away from his room for a short time his favorite violin, a Stradivarius, was stolen. The inspector took immediate action and, through diligent research, was able to identify four suspects. Each of them makes one statement as follows. The guilty one's statement is false; the other statements are true.

A. I was not in town at the time of the theft.
B. C is the culprit.
C. B's statement is false.
D. C's statement is true.

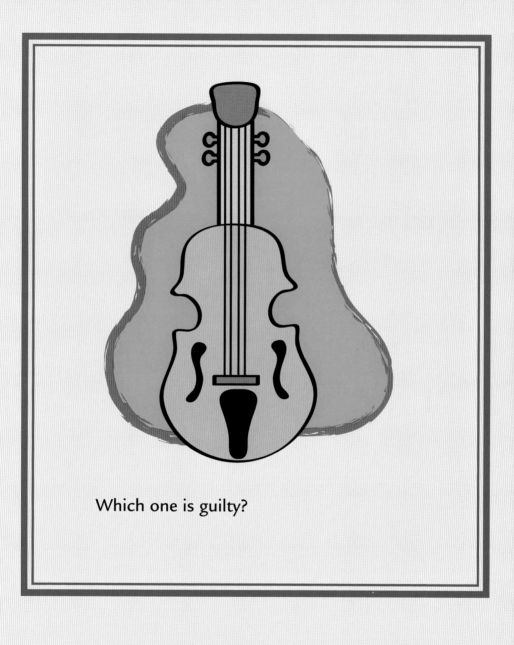

Which one is guilty?

The Forest Robber

A notorious robber has made a lucrative living by robbing travelers in the forest. Inspector Detweiler has, after extensive examination of the available clues, identified three suspects. Their statements follow. One makes two true statements; one makes one true and one false statement; one makes two false statements.

A. 1. I am not the robber.
    2. C is the robber.
B. 1. C is innocent.
    2. A is the robber.
C. 1. I am not the robber.

Which one is the robber?

Nonsense

Here are two puzzles that may seem absurd and may not rely on any facts of which we have knowledge. There is logic in them, however, if you can assume that the statements are valid. Can you uncover the inference in each puzzle?

Rabbits Play Hockey

1. Some alligators carry umbrellas in the shower.
2. Only those that know that flying fish live in the trees prefer caramel candy to chocolate.
3. Certain days are set aside for alligators to watch rabbits play hockey.
4. Some large reptiles are steeplechasers.
5. Only steeplechasers can watch hockey games.

6. Those alligators that carry umbrellas in the shower know that flying fish live in the trees.
7. Those that prefer chocolate to caramel candy cannot be steeplechasers.
8. Steeplechasers are vegetarians.

What inference can you draw from the above statements?

Gorillas Enjoy Ballet

1. Gorillas are the only animals that enjoy ballet.
2. All animals can fly to Mars.
3. Scotch broom blooms every Thursday all over Mars.
4. Only those few animals that do not play solitaire are immune to hay fever.
5. No animal that travels in leaky rowboats ever has the penultimate word in a verbal discourse.
6. Scotch broom in bloom is what gives animals severe hay fever.

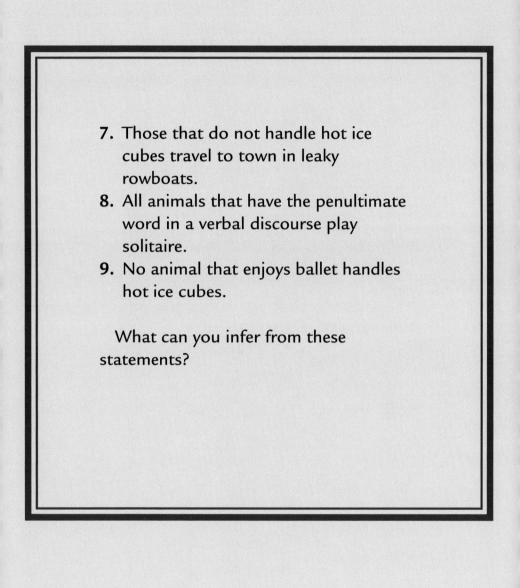

7. Those that do not handle hot ice cubes travel to town in leaky rowboats.

8. All animals that have the penultimate word in a verbal discourse play solitaire.

9. No animal that enjoys ballet handles hot ice cubes.

What can you infer from these statements?

BrainSnack™ Puzzles
Answers

Page 10
Landscape A does not belong.

Page 11
Piece number 2.

Page 12
Three. The sum of the figures of the year equals the
number of glasses of eggnog the skier had.

Page 13
A, B, and D. If you add C and/or E to the other
lollipops, you end up with eight different flavors.

Page 14
After four skewers, the order of the pieces of meat is
repeated: ABCDABC, DABCDAB, CDABCDA,
BCDABCD. The 100th skewer will follow the fourth
order of meat (4 x 25=100). That is why the 99th

skewer will be the third-order combination—i.e.,
CDABCDA.

Page 15
5. Starting at 2 and going clockwise, the sequence of
numbers is carried out by +1, +2, +3, +4, +5.

Page 16
Liquid 4. The liquid with the highest density is to be
found at the bottom of the test tube. Here you have
the liquids in order of density: 1, 3, 5, 2, 4.

Page 17
20. Starting with the first number (4), the sequence
of numbers is carried out by x1, −2, x3, −4, x5, −6,
x7, −8.

Page 18
820969371. It is clear that only the number 0 is
correctly reproduced. When you enter one of the other
numbers, the two accompanying numbers in the same
column appear on the display. For instance, if you enter
the number 5, then 82 will be shown on the display.

Page 19
Print E. The middle line has shifted.

Page 20
Cube number 3.

Page 21
ACE.

Page 22
All five piece fit perfectly into the block. But piece number 2 is the only one that has the correct colors.

Page 23
Cube 2. The blue frame on the top side should be orange in order for the cube to be identical with the original cube.

Page 24
Dais 2. The cube at the far right does not match the layout.

Page 25
Ribbon number 3 is wrong.

Page 26
1-3, 2-6, 4-5. The design patterns are the same on the right and left skis of each pair.

Page 27
351. The numerical position of a letter in the alphabet tells you the number of egg lifts corresponding to that letter. For example, A corresponds to one lift, B to two lifts, and so on until 26 egg lifts for the letter Z. In total, the lift will have 351 eggs.

Page 28
Snowboard 3. On all the other snowboards, the word "HOT" is the same color as the big star and the triangle is the same color as the small star.

Page 29
24B. The pin code is found using this formula: The digit is 26 minus the number. The letter is the place of the number in the alphabet. For example: The pin code for 8 is 26 – 8 = 18, and the eighth letter of the alphabet, H: 18H.

Page 30
(6,6). The line of the graph connects only those points of which the values are labeled correctly. On the horizontal axis those values are 0, 2, 3, 5, and 6. On the vertical axis they are 0, 1, 4, and 6. The only point that remains to connect is (6,6).

Page 31
091. Each number is the second digit of the sum of the other numbers in the same column. In the first column, 9 + 1 + 0 = 10, and we keep the 0. The second column: 8 + 9 + 2 = 19, and we keep the 9. And finally, 4 + 0 + 7 = 11, and we keep the 1.

Page 32
5. All the other servings have as many olives as they have slices of cold cuts.

Page 33
7. Every snowman has the same number of buttons on its face as on its body.

Page 34
3. The number of the berries and leaves always totals 8.

Page 35
9, J, 11, and 12. The points go in numerical order from 1 to 29. Each fifth point is replaced by the letter of the alphabet that occupies that numerical position.

Page 36
Slice number 6 is from the third cake because the cherry is in the middle of the cake.

Page 37
Wrapping number 5. In order for it to be identical with the other wrappings, the green side should be purple.

Page 38
4. All the other coats of arms use the same three colors. Coat 4 only uses two colors.

Page 39
Stack C. In all the other stacks, the order of the colors is yellow, light green, gray, white, and pink.

Page 40
6. Sets 2 and 8 tell you that the red block has not been threaded.

Page 41
RU (right upper). All the arrows are part of smaller or larger endless loops.

Page 42
Mask number 4. In all the other masks, the right eye
has moved 180° in relation to the left eye.

Page 43
Flag number 8. The left part of each flag has the color
sequence black, blue, yellow, and red. The right part
has the color sequence red, white, and black. So the
right half of flag number 8 should be white.

Page 44
22. The number of the next shorts is the number of
the previous shorts plus the number in the black
rectangle.

Page 45
20. The sum of the numbers of the same-colored
chairs is always 25.

Page 46
Cap number 3. To have made cap number 3 would
have taken five different fabrics.

Page 47
7. Each number represents the number of identically colored soccer balls.

Page 48
Object number 2.

Page 49
Design 4. All the other designs have a red ring at the bottom.

Page 50
92. A silver medal costs 320 (2142 − 1822). A gold medal costs 1502 (1822 − 320). Consequently, the bronze medal costs 1914 − 320 − 1502 = 92.

Page 51
B3.

Page 52
Three. The difference between the number of black and white dots is always two. The last ladybug should have three white dots.

Page 53
Wheel B will turn to the left (counterclockwise).

Page 54
10. The row of cells follows the color sequence red, orange, and lavender. Cell number 10 does not follow that sequence.

Page 55
Pile 3. Brian's piles follow a color scheme: Orange, green, and blue always succeed each other in the same order. In doing so, he has considered both the front and side of the piles. The only pile he can put his last present on is pile 3.

Page 56
Cube 2.

Page 57
Stamp C is the only stamp in which the little square does not have the same color as its background.

Page 58
$8100. Each time the price drops by 10%.

Page 59
*All three patterns can be made with this tile. Imagine
a ticktacktoe box over each pattern and you will see
how the tile fits.*

Page 60
*F. At each T-intersection, the marathon runner makes
a right. At each circular point, he goes to the left,
and, at each crossroad, he runs straight. Following this
pattern, the runner will be leaving the city at point F.*

Page 61
*2. The only flavor his usual store does not have is
vanilla.*

Page 62
*O. In our alphabet, ten letters are their own mirror
image. Therefore, the missing letter is O.*

Page 63
Row H and column 4. The vertical bars move one step to the right per screen, and the horizontal bars two steps down. The last screen should show the vertical bar in position 4 and the horizontal line in position H.

Page 64
Track D. The red buoy must be taken on the left-hand side and the yellow buoy on the right-hand side.

Page 65
7. The score is equal to the total number of marks plus the marks put inside the small square.

Page 66
22. $b = x + 1$, $b + x = c$; so $x + 1 + x = c$ or $c = 2x + 1$. $c + x = d$; so $2x + 1 + x = d$ or $d = 3x + 1$. $d + x = 89$; so $3x + 1 + x = 89$. To solve for x: $4x + 1 = 89$, $4x = 88$, $x = 22$.

Page 67
Ladybug number 2.

Page 68
April. The number of chocolate lines on the cakes indicates the month.

Page 69
8. The sum of each row and each column equals 15.

Page 70
6, 9, and 8. The numbers are alternately added and subtracted: 2 + 3 = 5; 5 − 1 = 4; 4 + 6 = 10, etc.

Page 71
Move the fourth chalk line in order to end up with the square root of one. $\sqrt{1} = 1$.

Page 72
74. Each number is the sum of the number in the previous row plus the product of its digits: 13 + (1 x 3), 16 + (1 x 6), 22 + (2 x 2), 26 + (2 x 6), 38 + (3 x 8), 62 + (6 x 2) = 74.

Page 73
Switch lightbulbs F and G and the color sequence is blue, yellow, and red.

Page 74
3. The sum of the yellow and blue lights equals the number of red lights.

Page 75
6 dots.

Page 76
9362. With all the other numbers, the first two and the last two digits always add up to ten.

Page 77
B. At each intersection where there are four red rooftops, the messenger goes straight. At each intersection where there are four gray rooftops, he turns left; at four green rooftops, he turns right. Following this pattern, he will leave the city at point B.

Page 78
6. Follow a spiral that unfolds towards the center.

Page 79
2. The figure inside each square has the color of the preceding square.

Page 80
Elements 1 and 2.

Page 81
From bottom to top: 311222. The most same-colored blocks are stacked on top.

Page 82
77798. All the numbers can be read as follows: 89 90 9(1), 69 70 7(1), 28 29 3(0), etc.

Page 83
4. The color of the thick lines is different from the color of the bottom triangle.

Page 84
7. The number on the cap is the sum of the numbers of the neighboring lanes: 2 + 5 = 7.

Page 85
Piece A.

Page 86
480/360. The numerator and denominator of each fraction are multiplied by their position in the series. The product of the numerator becomes the denominator in the next fraction and the product of the denominator becomes the numerator in the next fraction. To get the last fraction of the series, the numerator (72) of the fifth fraction is multiplied by its position (5) to give you the denominator of the next fraction. The denominator (96) is multiplied by its position (5) to give you the numerator of the next fraction.

Page 87
*1321123113. Each line is a literal translation of the
contents of the previous line. For example: To get the
numbers of the second line, the previous line has one
1, one 2, and one 3—or, 111213. The next line has
three 1s, one 2, one 1, and one 3—or, 31121113.
For the last line, we have one 3, two 1s, one 2, three
1s, and one 3: 1321123113.*

Page 88
*4. From the first operation, it appears red is the
dominant color. From the second operation, it appears
that, apart from the color red, the cube is the
dominant shape. Consequently, the third operation
will produce a red cube.*

Page 89
*78. The numbers around 5 and 2 move forward one
position clockwise. Therefore, 89 will show up as 78
on the screen.*

Great Color Optical Illusions Answers

Page 92

At first glance, you see a bearded man. On closer inspection, you'll find a phoenix.

Page 92

The zebra is descended from a solid black animal. The white stripes are superficial tufts on the black background color of the animal's skin.

Page 93

The drum appears to spin. The word "rotator" is a palindrome; it reads the same backwards and forwards.

Page 94
The old lady's face shows her life. You can see her as a baby, a young girl, courting, in marriage, and finally in death. This type of art is based on the work of Archimboldo, a painter who lived in Italy from 1517 to 1593.

Page 95
Turn the page upside down to see them smiling. Now they are married.

Page 96
The young woman's chin becomes the nose of the old lady.

Page 97
Bring the page close to your face. The bee and flower will come together.

Page 97
The circle appears to be in two different shades of color.

Page 98
The Three of Hearts (tree of hearts).

Page 99
Mona Lisa.

Page 100
Look closely and you'll find the profiles of Adam and Eve. The phrase "Madam I'm Adam" is a palindrome; it reads the same backwards and forwards.

Page 101
It looks like an old Asian man. Daniel Webster's shirt forms his forehead.

Page 101
The letter E. Try looking at the page from a distance.

Page 102
The secret word is "hello." Look at the page in the direction of the arrow at eye level.

Page 103
It changes direction!

Page 104
Turn the page upside down and you will see a slice of cake. The name "Otto" has both horizontal and vertical symmetry. And it's also a palindrome!

Page 105
They are both the same size. Trace one of them and measure it against the other. Their curve tricks us and creates the illusion.

Page 106
It is a magic square. Each horizontal, vertical, and diagonal line of four numbers adds up to 264. It also works if you turn it upside down.

Page 107
It all depends on how you look at it.

Page 107
It's a crate. Look at the illustration. It's easier to see it with the added lines.

Page 108
A black cat down a coal mine eating a stick of licorice at midnight.

Page 108
Pile B. Were you surprised? Measure each of them to check.

Page 109
Turn the page upside down.

Page 110
Each circle will seem to revolve on its axis. The inner cog wheel will appear to rotate in the opposite direction.

Page 110
The message, made up from the pale background shapes, says, "Can you find the words."

Page 111
It appears to follow you, but it's just an illusion. This design was used as a recruiting poster for the British Army.

Page 111
Turn the page upside down and you will see the mother's head. The baby's diaper becomes the mother's head scarf.

Page 112
The face can belong to either the man or the woman.

Page 113
Turn the page upside down.

Page 114
The right eye and bridge of the nose form the heads of Romeo and Juliet. This form of art was popular in the 19th century in Europe.

Page 115
A part of Hearn's act is shown close-up. From a distance, it resembles the performer.

Page 116
Look at the reflection of this page in the mirror.

Page 116
It says, "We see but we we don't observe."

Page 117
A person riding a horse. See the illustration.

Page 118
Take your pick!

Page 119
The choice is yours. It all depends on what you saw first. Horizontally, it reads A, B, C. Vertically, it reads 12, 13, 14.

Page 119
The choice is yours!

Page 120
Turn the page upside down. Then look at the reflection in a mirror and you will see the correct price is only 20¢.

Page 120
Bring the page closer to your face. The figures will come together.

Page 121
Look at the left side of the picture and you will see the profile of the farmer's face.

Page 121
Look at the markings on the cow's back. You will see a map of the United Kingdom.

Page 122
It says, "I've got a a big head."

Page 123
There are six F's in the sentence.

Page 124
Turn the page 90° counterclockwise.

Page 125
See the illustration.

Page 126
"X" marks their spot. See illustration.

Page 127
*Turn the page 90° counterclockwise. His face will
appear.*

Page 128
*Napoleon's silhouette is found between the two trees
on the right.*

Page 129
*Look at the lion's mane. You will see some of the old
British colonies: Canada, India, Australia, New
Zealand, and African colonies.*

Page 130
*It is supposed to be the longest sentence that still reads
the same when you turn it upside down.*

Page 131
*The three donkeys have only three ears
among them!*

Page 131
Your guess is as good as mine. It's impossible to tell.

Page 132
Look at the sequence of the words. It says,
"the with." It should be "with the."

Page 133
The choice is yours. Did you notice that the caption
says, "How many can can you see?"

Page 134
The middle leg is impossible.

Page 135
Turn on the light. It's an impossible candelabra. A
number of the holders seem to be suspended in midair.

Page 136
Turn the page upside down and it says, "Lots
o' eggs."

Page 137
The previous one was 1881. The next one will occur in the year 6009.

Page 138
To tie mules to.

Page 138
The shapes spell the word "eye." The shelf is an impossible object.

Page 139
It says, "Optical illusions are magic."

Page 140
You will see a lightbulb with a glowing yellow center. Yellow is the reverse color to blue. These opposite colors are known as complementary colors.

Page 141
Turn the page 90° clockwise to reveal the circus.

Page 142
It depends on what direction you see the bird flying.
Either answer is correct.

Page 143
Study the picture carefully and you'll see his face. His
hat is formed from the dog's ear.

Page 144
It's a dog curled up on a rug. Turn the page so that the
arrow points upwards to reveal the dog.

Page 145
The blue dot that is on the line is in the center.

Page 146
Yes, it's impossible. Count the number of steps. You
can count three, nine, or five steps.

Page 147
You might see a medal or two people having
an argument.

Page 147
The star is midway between the point and the base.
Use a ruler and you'll see.

Page 148
They are both the same height. The lines of
perspective help to create the illusion of one being
taller than the other.

Page 148
No. The set of stairs is impossible.

Page 149
At first glance, we think he's happy. But he's really
sad. We are not used to seeing faces upside down.
Since the mouth and eyes have been inverted, he
seems very weird when we look at him.

Page 150
The fourth one down reads "something."

Page 151
Turn the page upside down and he looks exactly the same.

Page 151
Turn the page 90° counterclockwise.

Page 152
From a distance, it's a skull. Close up, it's a man and woman sitting at a table.

Page 153
Turn the page upside down for the answer. It says "Life."

Page 153
Slowly bring the page closer to your face. At a certain point, the matches will join up.

Page 154
It says, "The end."

Sneaky Lateral Thinking Puzzles Clues

Page 156
He lived a lonely life in a remote building. He made the statue out of copper. It was taken far away and he never saw it again. He died as the result of an accident. No other person or animal or sculpture was involved.

Page 157
The man died in an accident. He was not poisoned or stabbed. No other person was involved. No crime was involved. The man did not eat the fish. The type of fish is irrelevant. It was dead. He was not indoors.

Page 158
There was no one else around. The foreign visitor saw
a sign. He was very obedient.

Page 159
It was not a good shot that got him the hole in one.
He should have been more careful. The golfer's ball
rebounded into the hole. Another person was involved.

Page 160
He is not trying to form words or to communicate or
send a message. The man is working on a crossword
puzzle. The letters he writes are S and E.

Page 161
The blunder did not involve physics, chemistry,
mathematics, or astronomy. The blunder concerned
the twins, Viola and Sebastian.

Page 162
The same environmental change would have occurred
if felt hats or woolen hats had become very popular.
More silk hats were sold and fewer other hats were
sold. Fur hats were out of fashion.

Page 163
Aeschylus did not trip over the tortoise or slip on it.
He did not eat it or attempt to eat it. He was not
poisoned or bitten by the tortoise. No other human
was involved in his death.

Page 164
Driving conditions were excellent, but the thief found
the woman's car very difficult to drive. She had had
the car modified. The rich woman suffered from some
of the same frailties as other old people. There was
nothing unusual about the car's engine, gears, wheels,
steering, or bodywork.

Page 165
Leonardo hid the designs in a place where he thought nobody would ever find them, but they were not buried or locked away. People carefully stored the hidden designs for years without realizing they had them.

Page 166
She didn't know the men and didn't like any of them. She had malicious intentions. There was potential financial gain for her.

Page 167
There were many trees along the side of the road. The man had never seen or noticed this tree before. There was something different about this tree. His primary concern was safety. The tree itself was not a threat to him.

Page 168
The café owner did not change the menu or prices or music in the café. He changed the appearance of the café in a way that embarrassed the teenagers.

Page 169
No other person or animal was involved. The change in color was not caused by the sun or wind. The change in color was caused by the rain, but every other house and fence in the area remained unchanged in color.

Page 170
Do not take this puzzle too seriously—it involves a bad pun. The child was correct. But why?

Page 171
The fact that he is religious is not relevant. The vicar is particular about his appearance.

Page 172
The wristwatch was perfectly legal and did not give the
runner an unfair advantage. The man had cheated.
The clue to his cheating was that his wristwatch had
changed hands.

Page 173
They were deliberately cast adrift from a famous boat.
The animals can sometimes offend the senses.

Page 174
She was strangled to death with a scarf. No dancing
was involved. She should not have been in such a
hurry.

Page 175
The tomato fell six feet. It was a regular tomato. The
man was fast.

Page 176
The shopkeeper could easily change the sign, but
chooses not to do so. No superstition about numbers is
involved. Many people notice the discrepancy.

Page 177
The shoes fit him comfortably, but there was
something uncomfortable about them. They were
made of different material from his other shoes. They
were fine when worn outside, but not when worn
inside.

Page 178
It was a long process. Somebody helped him. He used
a part of his body that was not paralyzed.

Page 179
The girl is very sad. She is trying to prevent something
from happening. She is acting on something she heard.

Page 180
She was in her home when this happened. She had heard the tune many times before. Normally she was happy when she heard this tune. The stranger was trying to rob her.

Page 181
The police officer was perfectly capable of chasing the teenagers and he was not engaged in any other task at the time. The officer was conscientious and always chased and apprehended those he saw breaking the law.

Page 182
The second orange goes under the first orange but the first orange remains on the table.

Page 183
She was chosen on merit. She was a good typist.

Page 184
The T-shirts were designed to circumvent the law. The law was a traffic regulation. The black band was a diagonal stripe.

Page 185
The man is very skillful in his use of the stick. The man strikes something made of ivory.

Page 186
Although he constructed it with great care, the man thought that the house might fall down. He didn't intend that he or anyone else live in the house.

Page 187
The meteorologist died. He wasn't aware of the stuffed cloud. It hadn't affected any of his forecasts or reports. He was traveling.

Page 188
The bird was just as beautiful and rare as he had imagined. He wasn't disappointed with its appearance. What happened to the bird placed him at risk. He saw the bird through a small window.

Page 189
The horse was alive throughout and was not exceptional. The horse was a working horse. The two legs that traveled farthest were the front left and back left.

Page 190
They weren't playing strip poker and stripping wasn't a forfeit or penalty involved in the game. The actual card game isn't relevant. She took off her clothes to avoid harm.

Page 191
They were sold on the same day at the same market. Each was sold for a fair price. The two pigs looked the same, but when they were sold one was worth much more than the other. One was sold for food—the other was not.

Page 192
The man was physically fit and healthy. The feather had touched him. He was a circus performer.

Page 193
He was embarrassed with shame when his gift was opened. His gift wasn't offensive to the bride and groom in any religious, political, or moral way. He had bought an expensive gift but then made a mistake and tried to save money.

Page 194
Adam did not use the hammer on the computer. The computer was undamaged. Brenda had a disability.

Page 195
This is not a fashion issue. It has to do with right- and left-handedness. When buttons first came into use, it was the better-off who used them.

Page 196
The frogs were physically identical. One managed to survive the ordeal because of the result of its actions. The nature of the liquid is important.

Page 197
The butterfly was not a live butterfly. The man walked into trouble. The model butterfly served as a warning.

Page 198
He was not interested in the time. He wanted to make an innocuous telephone call. He was cheating.

Page 199
He wanted the cat to do something for him.

Page 200
The man was a movie star. The people who lost their jobs worked in the garment industry.

Page 201
The New York hairdresser had nothing against New Yorkers and has no particular love of Canadians. He charges everyone the same price for one haircut.

Page 202
Twelve men had started out in the attempt to become king. The one who succeeded was one of the few to survive.

Page 203
His performances were always a flop, but he was very successful. He was not in comedy, music, cinema, or theater. His most famous performance was in Mexico. He was a sportsman.

Page 204
It is not underwater—it is clearly visible aboveground.
It would be very difficult to climb.

Page 205
They used regular water. The road was not
contaminated in any way. It was for a special event.
They did not hose the entire road.

Page 206
The restaurant is in an unusual location.

Page 207
She had good intentions. He was in danger.

Page 208
The mother lures the insect out of her daughter's ear.

Sneaky Lateral Thinking Puzzles Answers

Page 156
He lived in a tower on a hill. Being poor, he had no money for materials, so he took the copper lightning rod from the building. He made a beautiful statue with the copper, but soon afterward the tower was struck by lightning and he was killed.

Page 157
The man's boat had capsized and he was adrift in an inflatable dinghy in a cold ocean. He caught a fish and, while cutting it up, his knife slipped and punctured the dinghy.

Page 158
The foreign visitor saw a sign saying, "Dogs must be carried." He did not have a dog!

Page 159
The golfer's ball rebounded off the head of another golfer who was crossing the green. The ball bounced into the hole. However, the man who was hit died.

Page 160
The man is given the world's most difficult crossword and offered a prize of $100 for every letter he gets right. He puts "S" for each initial letter and "E" in every other space. S is the commonest initial letter and E the commonest letter in the English language.

Page 161
The identical twins Viola and Sebastian are different sexes. This is impossible.

Page 162
Because silk hats came into fashion, the demand for beaver hats decreased. More beavers meant more small lakes and bogs.

Page 163
Aeschylus was killed when the tortoise was dropped on him from a height by an eagle who may have mistaken the bald head of Aeschylus for a rock on which to break the tortoise.

Page 164
The rich woman was very nearsighted, but did not like wearing glasses or contact lenses. So she had her windshield ground to her prescription. The thief could not see clearly through it.

Page 165
Leonardo hid the secret designs by painting over them with beautiful oil paintings. He knew that no one would remove such masterpieces. But he did not know that modern X-ray techniques would allow art historians to see through the oil paintings and reveal his designs.

Page 166
She was a divorce lawyer drumming up business!

Page 167
The man saw a tree lying across the road. He was in Africa and he knew that blocking the road with a tree was a favorite trick of armed bandits, who then waited for a car to stop at the tree so that they could ambush and rob the passengers. He guessed correctly that this was the case here, so he reversed quickly to avoid danger.

Page 168
The café owner installed pink lighting that highlighted all the teenagers' acne!

Page 169
The man had made green paint by mixing yellow paint and blue paint. The blue paint was oil-based, but the yellow paint was water-based. Heavy rain had dissolved the yellow paint, leaving the fence decidedly blue.

Page 170
The child was correct. It was a mail train!

Page 171
The vicar wears black suits and knows that light-colored dog hairs will show up on his suits, but that black ones will not be noticed.

Page 172
A picture of the runner early in the race showed him wearing his watch on his right wrist. When he crossed the finishing line, it was on his left wrist. The judges investigated further and found that one man had run the first half of the race and his identical twin brother had run the second half. They had switched at a toilet on the route.

Page 173
The two animals were skunks that had been ejected from Noah's Ark because of the stench they were causing.

Page 174
The famous dancer was Isadora Duncan, who was strangled when the long scarf she was wearing caught in the wheel of her sports car.

Page 175
He caught it just above the ground.

Page 176
It was originally a mistake, but the shopkeeper found that so many people came into his shop to point out the error that it increased his business.

Page 177
The man found that the synthetic shoes generated a buildup of static electricity when he wore them around his carpeted office. He constantly got electric shocks, so he rejected them and went back to his old leather shoes.

Page 178

He winked one eye and thereby indicated to a very dedicated assistant each letter, word, and sentence of the book. He was Jean-Dominique Bauby, the French writer. The book he wrote by blinking, The Diving Bell and the Butterfly, was published just before his death in 1996 and became a best-seller.

Page 179

The girl has a fatal disease. She overheard the doctor tell her mother that by the time all the leaves have fallen from the trees she will be dead.

Page 180

The woman was alone and asleep in her house in the middle of the night when she was awakened by the sound of her musical jewel box. She knew that a burglar was in her bedroom. She reached under her pillow, pulled out a gun, and shot him.

Page 181
The teenagers were traveling on the road that crossed the road the police officer was on. They drove through a green light.

Page 182
Put it under the table.

Page 183
Typing eleven words per minute is going quite fast, if the language is Chinese!

Page 184
A law was introduced making the wearing of seat belts compulsory for car drivers and passengers. Many Italians tried to circumvent the law. They wore the T-shirts in order to give the false impression that they were wearing seat belts.

Page 185
The man is playing billiards (or snooker or pool) with balls made of ivory. By pocketing a ball with his cue, he wins the match.

Page 186
The man was building a house of cards.

Page 187
A stuffed cloud, in pilot slang, is a cloud with a mountain in it. The meteorologist was a passenger on a plane that hit a stuffed cloud. He was killed and had to be replaced at his job.

Page 188
The ornithologist was sitting on a plane coming in to land when he saw the rare bird, which was sucked into the jet engine causing the engine to fail and the plane to crash-land.

Page 189
The horse worked in a mill. It walked around in a circle all day to drive the millstone. In the course of the day, its outer legs walked a mile farther than its inner legs.

Page 190
When one player went to play a card, she knocked over a mug. The hot drink poured over the other player, who immediately jumped up and started to take her clothes off.

Page 191
This happened in France. One pig was sold for bacon. The other had been painstakingly trained to sniff out truffles and was, therefore, very valuable.

Page 192
The man was a circus sword swallower. In the middle of his act someone tickled him with the feather and he gagged.

Page 193
The man selected a beautiful crystal vase in a gift shop, but he knocked it over and broke it. He had to pay for it, so he instructed the shop to wrap it and send it anyway. He assumed that people would think that it had been broken in transit. Unfortunately for him, the shop assistant carefully wrapped every broken piece before sending the package.

Page 194
Brenda was blind and she depended on her Braille manual when using the computer. Alan flattened the pages with a hammer.

Page 195
*Most people are right-handed and find it easier to
fasten a button which is on the right through a hole
which is on the left. This is why men's buttons are on
the right. When buttons were first used it was the
better-off who could afford clothes with buttons.
Among this class the ladies were often dressed by
maid-servants. The servant would face the lady, and so
it was easier for right-handed servants to fasten
buttons that were on the lady's left.*

Page 196
*The frogs fell into a large tank of cream. One swam
around for a while but then gave up and drowned. The
other kept swimming until his movements turned the
cream into knobs of butter, on which he safely floated.*

Page 197
*The butterfly was made of plastic and was put on a
large plate-glass window to indicate the presence of
the glass. After it fell off, a man walked into the
window and was seriously injured.*

Page 198
The man is having an affair. Once he has phoned his mistress, he calls the clock so that if his wife should later press the redial button she will not find out anything he does not want her to know.

Page 199
The man was a television cable engineer who needed to thread a cable from the back of a house, under the floor, to the front. He released the cat with a string attached to it into a hole at the back of the house. The cat was lured by the smell of the cream and salmon to find its way under the floor to the front of the house. The string was used to pull the cable through.

Page 200
The man was Clark Gable, the screen idol, who took off his shirt in a movie in which he was about to go to bed. He was not wearing an undershirt. So great was his influence that men stopped wearing undershirts and factories making them had to close down. In a

later movie, he wore an undershirt and restored it to fashion.

Page 201
He gets three times as much money!

Page 202
This is normal in a game of checkers (or draughts).

Page 203
His name was Dick Fosbury, inventor of the famous Fosbury flop, a new high-jumping technique that involved going over the bar backward and that revolutionized the sport. He won the gold medal in the Mexico City Olympics in 1968.

Page 204
The largest-known extinct volcano is Mons Olympus on Mars.

Page 205
This incident occurred just before the start of the
Monaco Grand Prix race, which is held in the streets
of Monte Carlo. Part of the course runs through a
tunnel. When it rains outside, the firemen hose down
the road in the tunnel in order to make the surface
wet. This improves consistency and safety.

Page 206
It is the first-class restaurant on a luxury ocean liner.
Upstairs is out on deck. If it rains the entire company
transfers downstairs and takes up where it left off.

Page 207
He was holding a live electric cable. The electricity had
paralyzed the muscles in his arm. Her action freed
him.

Page 208
She put the girl in a darkened room and placed a
bright light near her ear. The insect emerged.

Clever Logic Puzzles Answers

Dragons of Lidd and Wonk

Page 215
One Dragon
The dragon is a rational.

Page 217
Two Dragons
A is a red rational. B is a gray predator.

Page 218
Three Dragons
A is a gray rational. B is a red rational.
C is a blue predator.

Page 221
Two Are from Wonk
A is a blue predator. B is a gray rational. C is a blue predator.

Page 222
One Dragon from Wonk
A is a red rational. B is a blue predator. C is a red predator.

Page 225
Three Dragons Again
A is a red predator. B is a blue rational. C is a red rational.

Page 226
How Many Are Protected?
A is a blue predator. B is a red predator. C is a gray predator.

Page 229
Who Speaks for Whom?
A is a blue predator. B is a red predator. C is a red rational.

The Trials of Xanthius

Pages 234–235
The First Trial
Path A is the one to follow.

Pages 236–237
The Second Trial
Path B is the correct choice.

Pages 238–239
The Third Trial
Path C is the one to follow.

Pages 240–241
The Fourth Trial
Bridge C is the one to cross.

Problems from the Addled Arithmetician

Page 246

Addition, Six Digits

A	B	C	D	E	F
2	5	3	1	0	4
	4				5

	2	4	3	0
+	2	1	1	5
	4	5	4	5

Pages 248–49

Subtraction, Six Digits

A	B	C	D	E	F
5	0	4	2	1	3
		5	3	0	2

	3	0	5	4	0
−	2	5	3	1	0
		5	2	3	0

Page 251

Addition, Seven Digits

A	B	C	D	E	F	G
2	3	0	6	4	1	5
		1	5		0	6

	6	5	2	4	0
+	4	1	3	2	0
1	0	6	5	6	0

Pages 252–253

Addition, Seven Digits Again

A	B	C	D	E	F
	9		4	3	
4	8	1	3	2	0
	3	4	9	4	4
	3	4	9	4	4
+	3	4	9	4	4
1	0	4	8	3	2

Pages 254–255
Multiplication, Six Digits

A	B	C	D	E	F
5		1		2	
4	2	0	1	3	5

```
        1   5   2
    ×   2   1   2
        3   0   4
    1   5   2
3   0   4
─────────────────
3   2   2   2   4
```

Page 256
Subtraction, Seven Digits

A	B	C	D	E	F	G
0	6	3	1	5	2	4
		2		6	1	5

```
    6   1   3   0   6   2   6
−   5   5   6   4   5   0   5
─────────────────────────────
    5   6   6   1   2   1
```

The Land of Liars

Page 260
Two Inhabitants
It is afternoon; A is the Pemtru;
B is the Amtru.

Page 262
Two Inhabitants Again
It is morning; A is an Amtru;
B is a Pemtru.

Page 265
Two Inhabitants Once Again
It is morning; A is a Pemtru;
B is an Amtru.

Page 266
Three Inhabitants
It is morning; A is the Pemtru;
B and C are Amtrus.

Page 269
Three Inhabitants Again
It is afternoon; A and C are Pemtrus;
B is an Amtru.

The Cases of
Inspector Detweiler

Pages 272–273
Who Stole the Stradivarius?
B is the thief.

Pages 274–275
The Forest Robber
C is the robber.

Nonsense

Pages 278–279
Rabbits Play Hockey
Only alligators that are vegetarians are allowed to
watch rabbits play hockey.

Pages 280–281
Gorillas Enjoy Ballet
All animals can fly to Mars, but gorillas are among the few animals that should go there on Thursdays.